STUDIES IN FRENCH LITERATURE No. 10

General Editor
W. G. Moore
Fellow and Tutor of St. John's College, Oxford

MONTAIGNE: ESSAYS

by

F. P. BOWMAN
Associate Professor of French, The University of Pennsylvania

BARRON'S EDUCATIONAL SERIES, INC.
WOODBURY, NEW YORK

All inquiries should be addressed to:
Barron's Educational Series, Inc.
113 Crossways Park Drive
Woodbury, New York 11797

Library of Congress Catalog Card Number: 66-20076

Printed in the United States of America

Contents

Introduction

Montaigne is not an easy author. There is the problem of his language; words are spelt differently, and you have to change *o*s to *a*s and leave out or add an *s* to turn him into modern orthography. Some words have disappeared from French (e.g. *onc*, which means *never*) and still others have changed meaning (*aucun* means *some*, not *none*). A dictionary or footnotes can solve most of these problems. More complicated are those words which for Montaigne do not mean exactly what they mean for us; *nature* is one, and *et* is another. These difficulties are part of a larger historical problem. Montaigne is not our contemporary, did not live as we do and was not educated as we are. He was a sixteenth-century man, and his problems, concerns and patterns of thought are those of his century. There is not room in these pages to discuss Renaissance thought in detail, but we must warn against the false modernism involved in making Montaigne into a founding father of the United Nations, an eighteenth-century *philosophe*, or a nineteenth-century pessimist. To read him properly, you must develop the tools of a philologist; you must understand the text, linguistically and historically, and find out how the man thought and wrote. The present study is aimed at helping do that, first, by looking at who Montaigne was, what he read, and under what circumstances he wrote; then by examining certain aspects of the *Essais* in order to show how he thought; finally, by making some observations about how he organized and expressed these thoughts.

Montaigne was not a transcendent ahistorical thinker; he owed much to the books he read and the people with whom he conversed. Such is also true of this study—some of the books are mentioned in the bibliographical note; for the people, gratitude must be expressed to Samuel Danon and Roger and Nancy Porter.

PART I

Montaigne's Life—What he read —How he wrote

In a sense, you need to know almost nothing about Montaigne's life, because the *Essais* tell you everything; in another sense, for so autobiographical a work any outside information is pertinent and helpful. A few dates are of use; he was born in 1533 and died in 1592. Rabelais published *Pantagruel* the year before his birth, *Gargantua* the year after. Four years after he died, Descartes was born. He lived under the rule of François I, Henri II, Charles IX, Henri III, and finally his friend Henri IV—though he did not live to see le Vert Galant's triumphal entry into Paris. He saw the St. Bartholomew's massacre in 1572, but not the proclamation of the Edict of Nantes in 1598. So Montaigne lived during a period of religious and political strife; at these events he was a troubled spectator, and sometimes an active participant. He came from prosperous merchant stock, but his father had managed to enter the *noblesse de robe*—the judicial nobility—and acquire a country château. He spent his early youth being excellently educated at home (speaking only Latin), and then passed seven rather unhappy years at the Collège de Guyenne. His dissatisfaction stemmed from the curriculum and the teaching methods, though he studied under some famous scholars he later came to admire. He continued the traditional curriculum at Bordeaux, and did his law at Toulouse. He then took, or rather his father bought for him (before he reached the requisite age), his own judicial position, first in Périgueux and then, when that court was abandoned, in Bordeaux. The *Essais* are full of usually disparaging comments about his legal experiences; the evidence suggests he was a competent but not overly active judge. It was then that he became a close friend of Etienne de la Boétie, a Stoic humanist whose death in 1563 affected Montaigne deeply. Two years later he married Françoise de la Chassagne; he seems always to have approved of her, and never to have been excessively devoted to her. In 1568 his father died and he became proprietor of the château; three years later he resigned his legal post: 'For a long time already tired of his slavery to public duty, still in full force he came to rest on the breast of the wise virgins and, in peace

9

and security, will spend the rest of his days there . . . given over to his liberty, his tranquillity, his leisures.' In his famous tower he had his library installed, and on the whole there he did spend his remaining days. He did often travel, including one long trip through Germany and Switzerland to Italy, undertaken in part as a tourist and in part for medical reasons, several other trips to take the waters and still others for political reasons. He served two terms as mayor of Bordeaux, where he had to keep the city faithful to the king, unite its conflicting factions, and finally face the problem of the plague. Montaigne did the sensible thing—stayed out of town—though the nineteenth century held it against him. He became mayor against his will, fulfilled his functions well, and was glad when he could return to his tower. He was not an unimportant man; he was *gentilhomme de la chambre* to both the King of France and the King of Navarre (the latter post, at least, unsolicited); more importantly, he was known and admired by many of the leading intellectual figures of his time. We should not think of him as a Gascon squire scribbling in his village, a sort of provincial sage; he knew Paris well, he knew much of the rest of the world, and if he struck his neigh-bours as a nice country gentleman, the rest of France considered him a wise, sane and remarkable voice.

He became known as such largely because of his publications. In 1569 he brought out a translation of Raymond of Sebonde's *Natural Theology*; in 1571 he had published La Boétie's translations and poems. In 1580 appeared the first edition of the *Essais*, which met with unexpected success; a second appeared in 1582, after his travels, with some additions. Another edition in 1588 presented the first text of Book III and many additions to I and II; these are known as the B texts. He continued to add to them and in 1595, after his death, Marie de Gournay, a young admirer of his who had become his 'fille adoptive', aided by Pierre de Brach, brought out a much-augmented posthumous edition. Today's editors follow not this text but the Bordeaux text, which contains Montaigne's own additions and corrections to the 1588 edition; these additions are known as C. In any given essay of Books I and II, a large part of the text will be additions—B or C—and a serious student of Montaigne will want an edition which shows what layer a passage belongs to.

It is tempting to suggest that you read some Montaigne in English, heretical as this idea may be. Montaigne's French is not easy and it might be wise to try him at a natural rate of speed, and with the vision of the structure of an essay only a full comprehension of the language can give. Lest you be tempted to continue in English, though, read several translations, including not only such contemporary excellent ones as those of Donald Frame (the most reliable) or George Zeitlin (who offers a valuable preface), or the more traditional standby, Triechman, but also those two English classics, Florio's and Cotton's. Florio may have mistaken *poison* for *poisson*, but his Elizabethan English has the vigour and charm of Montaigne's Renaissance French, and it was Florio's Montaigne that Shakespeare probably knew. Generations of later Englishmen knew Cotton's, who provides an interesting contrast with the first. The differences in the translations should send you back to the French, understanding Montaigne's annoyance at the inadequate interpreters he had to use in interrogating his fascinating cannibals, and sharing his conviction that it is better to know things first-hand than through others. The difficulty of his language should lead you to do one very helpful thing—read some short passages carefully. If necessary, copy them out with plenty of empty space; grasp the meaning of every word and sentence, study how the sentences are organized within themselves and how they follow one another, how ideas develop, how Montaigne makes his transitions, what unstated assumptions underlie his assertions, trying all the while to see what sort of mind would think and write this way. Perhaps Montaigne should be read the way he himself read—at intervals, and brief stretches at a time—but he must definitely be chewed and digested. Plattard claimed that he could only be read fifteen minutes at a time; it would be more correct to say that he can only be read fifteen pages at a time, but several hours may profitably be spent on those pages.

We have strayed in a Montaigne-like fashion; let us return to the details of his life. Despite his travels and political activities, it was mostly a quiet, domestic life. Not that he seems to have been very preoccupied with the daughters his wife bore him—all except one died in infancy, and he could never remember exactly how many there were—nor indeed with domestic details; he was proud of his acquired indifference to questions of money. Rather, his was a life spent reading, writing to friends, and talking with neighbours. The reading we discuss elsewhere, so far as it affected the *Essais*, but we must remember that Montaigne also read for purely aesthetic reasons—not only storytellers such as Rabelais, but especially poetry, for which he had a fondness bordering on worship and where he enjoyed both Latins (classical, such as Horace or Catullus, and modern, such as Buchanan and Dorat) and French (where his preferences, Du Bellay and Ronsard, coincide with ours). His correspondence was probably voluminous, but less than forty letters have come down to us, and many of these are of a rather official nature (letters to kings and city councils tend to be preserved). Several of the essays take the form of letters—to Mme de Duras, Mme de Foix, etc., and they are all closer to the epistle than to any other antecedent literary genre.

Around 1577 Montaigne suffered from his first attack of gallstones, which were to torture him the rest of his life. Despite his distrust of doctors, he sought every remedy known at the time—to no avail. So during many of the years when he was writing the *Essais*, he was in occasional but intense physical agony. His gout or rheumatism, like-wise chronic, was probably easy enough to bear, but the stone, which he discusses at length in the *Essais*, by the intensity and intermittency of its pain, demanded of him a mental discipline which may in part explain his straightforwardness as an author. He finally died, of the quinsy, in 1592, according to one report at the elevation in the mass which was being celebrated in his room; he left a comfortable fortune to his one surviving daughter and his still surviving mother.

*   *   *

Montaigne was a well-read man. He may not have equalled Erasmus or Justus Lipsius in learning, but this was because he did not want to; he always avoided the affectation of pedantry. If he often hid his borrow-ing from other authors, it was not to claim their ideas were his own, but rather to avoid seeming too pretentiously learned. He says that reading meant for him not thorough study and absorption, but occasional leafing through old favourites or newly acquired volumes (we know that he did re-read extensively, for he adds quotes from certain texts in each edition of his *Essais*). He even claimed that to read more than an hour at a sitting exhausted him. But this very statement dispels any notion that Montaigne was a superficial student. He probably did not read books from cover to cover, nor did he very often grasp the total import, the over-all plan of what he read. There we can compare his global understanding of Raymond de Sebonde to his rather partial comprehension of Plato and Socrates; certain Platonic ideas and theses return again and again, whereas others are left aside. The pages he did read, however, he read meditatively and with great care. We know this not only from the borrowings he made, and from the impact of certain authors on his thought, but also because this is how he wanted his own *Essais* read. If further proof were needed, some volumes from his library have been refound, and they are at times covered with annotations, corrections, additional examples which support or con-tradict their author's thesis.

What, then, did he read? Students of Montaigne are forever in debt to Pierre Villey who painstakingly, by a thorough study of the *Essais*, attempted to reconstruct his library and, with its help, reconstruct the chronology of the *Essais*. Montaigne claims he owned a thousand volumes, a large library for his time, but the roundness of the figure makes it open to doubt. We cannot be sure that he read all the works he quotes, for he may well have borrowed the quotation from one of those popular Renaissance books of golden sentences and anecdotes collected from here and there, which even Erasmus authored and which Montaigne himself originally intended to produce. So Villey's conjectures remain conjectures, but he has established a list of some two hundred and fifty books Montaigne read, including the seventy-six of which we possess his copy.

Montaigne read primarily Latin authors, or Latin translations of Greek authors (for instance, he read Plato in Ficino's Latin translation). His favourites were Seneca, Virgil, Horace, Cicero, and the historians Livy, Tacitus, Caesar, Suetonius, not to mention Juvenal and Petronius. Of these, by far and away the most important is Seneca; indeed, some essays contain nothing much but Seneca. He often criticized Cicero, usually on stylistic grounds, but these criticisms date from the 1580 edition, whereas C contains many quotations or borrowings from Cicero's moral works; he overcame his dislike. We may be grateful that he early decided to imitate the Senecan amble rather than the Ciceronian period. Lucretius he placed slightly below Virgil, and valued not only for his exposition of Epicurean doctrine but even more for his anecdotal material. He still shared the medieval veneration for Virgil as a philosopher, but he had a stronger love for him as a poet.

Despite his father's excellent pedagogical methods—he taught Michel Greek pretending it was a game—Montaigne never mastered the other classical tongue. He quotes in the original Greek at times, but he paraphrases more often from translations, and his Greek quotes were probably lifted from anthologies. He read his favourite Greek author, Plutarch, in Amyot's translation for which he had an immense admiration only tempered when it was forcibly pointed out to him that the translation was far from accurate. He mentions Plutarch some seventy times, and quotes or borrows from him four hundred times! Most of these quotations come from the *Moralia* rather than the *Lives*. For Montaigne, Plutarch was above all the man who knew how to read history—how to get from it, not facts and dates, but those lessons of wisdom and morals he so highly valued; Plutarch was history already digested. After Plutarch, his favourite Greek author was Plato. He

showed his usual flair in labelling as spurious a dialogue most of the
Renaissance accepted as authentic. Whereas Plutarch's influence is
immense up to 1588 and declines in C, Socrates and Plato fascinate
Montaigne especially after 1588; there are many earlier references, but he
often then disputes or questions. With his own wisdom came a growing
appreciation of Socratic wisdom—and perhaps also of Socratic irony.
Herodotus he knew and admired as a repository of curious anthro-
pological data. Many facts came originally from Pliny the Elder, but
again were acquired through either translation or compilations. Sextus
Empiricus was put to great use in II, xii—the famous *Apologie*.

Before leaving the Latins and Greeks, it might be wise to say a few
words about Montaigne's evolution and the influence of these authors
on his thought. About Cicero he changed his mind; he borrows more
from Plato, less from Plutarch in his later years. We can date when he
read Caesar, which helps date some of the early essays. But usually he
returns again and again to a select, limited group of authors. He does
not move with adolescent enthusiasm from one guide to another, and
we should not speak of a Plutarch period followed by a Plato period, or
anything of the sort. From whom he borrows often depends on the
subject-matter he is discussing, not on the point he wants to make.
Moreover, before we describe any clear-cut evolution we must remember
that Montaigne always preferred authors who were tempered, whose
thought was not dogmatic but rather proffered with hesitations and
reservations. The one author he constantly refuses is Aristotle—in part
because Aristotle was the symbol of a medieval viewpoint he rejected,
in part because Aristotle was a systematic thinker, and Montaigne preferred the 'open form' and open mind of the Platonic dialogues. As
Zeitlin pointed out, when we speak of an evolution in Montaigne from
Stoicism to Epicureanism, we must remember that his major Stoic
source was Seneca, not Marcus Aurelius, and not only is C full of
Seneca but also Seneca was familiar with Epicureanism and hardly
presents Stoicism in an unadulterated form. Likewise, his main Epicurean
source is Lucretius, who has a rather Stoic 'native Roman austerity'
about him; and two-thirds of the Lucretian quotes come from B.

In this highly classical culture, the vernaculars played little if any
role. In French he read and quoted historians such as Commynes and
Joinville, or more rarely story-writers such as Bonaventure des Périers
and Rabelais. He does not seem to have known Dante except through
quotations made by others, and takes Boccaccio no more seriously than
he does Rabelais, but Castiglione seems to have exercised some influence
on his definition of the gentleman and on his notions concerning edu-

cation, and in politics he reacted intensely to Machiavelli's theses as the Renaissance understood them. On the whole, though, he uses vernacular sources either for the anecdotal material they contain, or else as anthologies from which he lifts thoughts in turn derived from the ancients.

Our habit of studying literatures according to the language in which they are written may give us a false picture of Montaigne. He may have read mostly Latin, but this does not mean that his culture was uniquely based on the great days of Greece and Rome. Erasmus, Ficino, Justus Lipsius were all Renaissance figures who wrote in Latin. These three are still well known, but we must also realize the importance for Montaigne of such authors as Cornelius Agrippa, whose volume on the uncertainty and vanity of science was used in the *Apologie*; Théodore de Bèze, not as a theologian but as a Latin poet; Michel de L'Hôpital, and many others now known primarily to historians of Renaissance thought. Montaigne was hardly indifferent to that thought. Indeed, he is rather unique in using the vernacular to express philosophical notions —Calvin, and even Descartes, still preferred Latin.

This library helps place Montaigne in his age. Despite his curiosity about cannibals and even Copernicus and despite the originality of his ideas about torture, tolerance and education, it is probably more enlightening to think of Montaigne as standing at the end of a tradition than to think of him as a pioneer. He builds on a heritage of thought which goes from the Renaissance humanists back to Homer. In this heritage he may pick and choose, but he thinks of himself as formed by past thinkers; he regards his intelligence as critical rather than as creative. Yet, his approach to his sources is quite different from that of the High Renaissance; he possesses no adulation for classical authors, does not hesitate to criticize them, does not feel that the antiquity of a source gives it any greater venerability. He is far removed from Petrarch's worship of the glories of Greece and Rome. He is not even particularly concerned with reading the classics accurately or thoroughly. No philologist, he willingly uses translations or anthologies. He himself translates freely, even to the point of wilfully mistranslating (changing *always* to *often*, etc.), and he happily quotes out of context. In II, x, he admits that when he encounters something he cannot understand, he reads on without bothering. In III, viii, he asserts that when he reads an author he looks for his *façon*, not his *sujet*; he wants to know the author, not to learn from him. He reads books the way he talks with people, so it is almost a matter of indifference *what* books he reads.

Even with his favourite sources, quite often he took some things from them, gladly leaving others behind. He is devoted to Plutarch because of what Plutarch has to say about the complexity of moral values and the variety of forces which influence man; he never pays much attention to Plutarch's praise of heroic virtue. In Plato, what interests him is what he can discover about the man Socrates, and little else. He does not accept Platonic ideals, nor the Platonic notions of immortality, and combats Renaissance Neoplatonism as much as he combats the Aristotelian system and its scholastic offspring. Socrates he admires as an anti-systematic thinker, and his picture of him owes something to Xenophon and Plutarch as well as to Plato. It was the Socratic emphasis on knowing yourself, not the conclusions of Socrates's self-knowledge, which fascinated him; so we must be very careful about what we mean when we call him a disciple of Plato. He certainly owed much to Epicurean thought, but here again he did not adopt Lucretius' scientific or cosmological theories. In all these classics, it is not the metaphysics which interest Montaigne, but the practical, moral conclusions. It is the incidental remark, and not the major thesis which strikes him. So his thought cannot properly be labelled Platonic, or Epicurean, or even less Stoic. Likewise, he reads history not for facts about the past, nor for historical theories, but for details and anecdotes which will enrich his picture of man.

Now Montaigne was not unique in picking and choosing details from various authors rather than identifying himself with any one school; this was a common Renaissance way (forecast already by Seneca) of showing the *personal* (as opposed to the *school*) nature of your culture. It was a natural technique for the open form he used in the *Essais*, which aims at inclusiveness rather than exclusiveness. It also had some important side-effects; Montaigne, for instance, is never concerned with reconciling classical antiquity with the truths of Christianity, not because he considers Christian dogma unimportant but because he does not think any Greek author could possess the sort of absolute validity which would bring him in conflict with it. Also, his picking and choosing enhances that lack of discrimination in the *Essais* which charms some and annoys others. All facts are valid, be they from Herodotus or Plato or Virgil, or be they from Montaigne's own daily experience of cleaning his teeth with his napkin. If he had been bent on digesting the complexity of Lucretius' thought he would probably not have gone so far in his portrait of the self. Montaigne, if he were seriously attacked for his high-handed manner of dealing with his sources, would reply in terms of his conviction of the universality of man; what he found in himself was bound to be in Lucretius, Plato and others, and he was primarily interested in them because they could contribute to the task of the *Essais*—testing and knowing himself.

This reasoning leaves unanswered the major question of why Montaigne read others and what function they served in elaborating his thought. Did he only find there corroboration—supporting quotations —for what he himself had already thought? If so, we can accuse him of using his cultural heritage as a sort of sonorous echo; indeed, we can accuse him of that pretentious pedantry of which he accused others. Yet, the most obviously personal and sincere essays—those most indebted to his own experience—are as full of references to other authors as any; the famous essay on friendship owes a great debt to Plato, Aristotle, Cicero, Castiglione, and so forth. This does not mean that Montaigne was ignorant of friendship himself and borrowed all his ideas on it from others, or that he personally exhausted the experience of friendship and then illustrated what he had to say by a few apt quotations. To limit him to these alternatives is to miss completely what he meant by conversation and what the Renaissance meant by imitation. At all moments, Montaigne's mind is in contact with others; even when he discusses housekeeping, what he says is influenced by Xenophon's *Œconomicus*. But that influence takes two forms—either a dialectic, or a formulation. In the dialectic, there is a movement between reading and experience, between his own ideas and the ideas of others, which enriches the content of his mind. He goes back and forth between his experience with La Boétie and the comments of *De amicitia* or the *Nicomachean ethics* to attain a deeper and more complete understanding of friendship. We cannot say that his reading substantiates his experience, nor that it uniquely shows him what to find in experience—for experience often shows him what to find in reading. Rather there was a subtle but enriching interchange between the two.

All literature is imitation, since it uses words which have been used by others in the sense in which they have used them. But Renaissance literature is consciously imitative in a much fuller way. The author of a Renaissance sonnet seeks in the tradition of the sonnet a means of formulating what he himself has to say. Montaigne's preference for open, rather than closed form, obviously exempts him from certain sorts of formal imitation, but other authors still aid him in the task of forming and expressing his thoughts. We might say he uses his sentences from Greek and Roman authors the way Ronsard uses the sonnet form, or the way certain modern philosophers use the language of mathematics. Reading not only enriched his thought, it also enriched the expression of that thought. So our post-Romantic categories of originality versus imitation do not apply, even though Montaigne rather suspected their existence. Exactly how imitation functioned in aiding expression will become clear when we come to discuss his style and his art as a story-teller.

*   *   *

Montaigne claims that he dictated, rather than wrote, at least the first draft of his *Essais*—while walking about in his book-lined study. Certainly the additions and corrections of the Bordeaux manuscript, made in his own handwriting, were done by himself, sitting at a desk. We may assume that this was also true of the B additions to I and II; probably even the A text, after it had been dictated, was revised by Montaigne, pen in hand. Many of the quotations must have been present in the first draft, for they are too well integrated to be later additions, and they organically serve to give impetus to his thought; they provide transitions or even the structure of the essay. The quotations and unquoted borrowings are of the very stuff of Montaigne.

Because of this method of composition, we should pay attention to the titles Montaigne gave the essays. We see him struck by a thought, or his mind working over some quotations, and probably as he began dictating the chapter he proposed a title for it. He may on occasion, as in 'Des Coches', have had an almost humorous intent, suggesting by his title what got him started rather than what the chapter is really about, but often the titles provide a hint to his central concern, and tell us much about how his mind is working If we can find out, through the chapter, what he means by *conscience* or *expérience* or *parsimonie*, or if we see why he considers 'la bataille de Dreux' of sufficient importance to make a title from it, then we have seen the point of the essay. That brief essay suggests that our temporary concerns should not distract us from our general goal; the three examples are military ones, and the two classical ones substantiate what had been observed in the battle at Dreux. Nor is the point as sententious as it may seem, because the battle of Dreux was 'tout plein de rares accidens', the way life, for Montaigne, was full of peculiar, unexpected events; the point is that the unexpected should not deflect us from reasonable conduct. This thesis was crystallized by a reminiscence, perhaps provoked through conversation ('ceux qui mettent volontiers en avant que . . .'), about the battle of Dreux. A natural enough process, which reminds us that Montaigne is very much concerned with military tactics. Thus his mind always moves between a particular incident and general observation.

The major problem is what, exactly, gave impetus to the thoughts of Montaigne? Here we must do some reconstruction. Conversation certainly played an important role; in his retreat he did not lead a solitary life, but conversed and corresponded with some of the best minds of his age. Also, he travelled. We must not think of Montaigne as someone annoyed with the world and embittered by La Boétie's death, sitting alone in his tower holding a schizophrenic soliloquy. He talked with others, wrote to others, and was exceptionally concerned with what they thought and how they reacted to what he thought. This is evident from his at times apologetic preoccupation with the reception the *Essais* are going to receive; it is even more evident in his friendship for Marie de Gournay, who seemingly only deserved his appreciation of her by her admiration for him. Mme de Foix is pregnant, and Montaigne is fond of her, and the result is an essay on how to raise and educate children; some other neighbour claims that the duc de Guise was a bad tactician, so the result is 'la bataille de Dreux'. Books undoubtedly provided the sort of impetus conversation provided, and in the same way. But only an examination of the content of the *Essais* can let us grasp what sort of a mind he had.

PART II

The 'Essais'

What, exactly, do the *Essais* say? They are too rich, too complex, and often too subtle to let us be exhaustive; indeed, we can only take some soundings which at best will suggest *how* Montaigne thought rather than *what* he thought, opening doors and pointing out especially how his mind differs from ours. First, we shall examine the problems involved in his effort to portray himself; then, his preoccupation with change (the *branle*), with the problem of causality, with the antithetical patterns he saw everywhere. Afterwards, we shall look briefly at what he said about nature (and what he meant by that word), death, religion and politics. But any categorizing of his thought is artificial; for instance, he did not originally intend to write autobiography and only came to do so because of his doubts about the possibility of knowing anything but the self. Also, the possibilities of self-knowledge are affected by the problem of change, and his fondness for antitheses determined in part the meaning he gave to *nature*. Montaigne rejected the categorizing tendencies of scholastic thought, and sought instead a kind of fluidity which makes him impossible to summarize, but impressively wise.

Autobiography

Reconstructing Montaigne's character at first seems an easy task, for in the later *Essais* his avowed goal was to paint himself. Certainly the picture he drew is present on almost every page. Detailed and extended portraits are given in I, xxvi; II, viii; x; xvii; and especially in III, ii, where he maintains that his self-portrait has a kind of universal validity. Other essays of III are full of autobiographical material. These portraits should be compared, for they not only complement each other but also differ in emphasis and lighting. To them should be added the many asides which are often just as revealing and perhaps more reliable. 'I said to him one day a bit hardily, as is my wont' gives us a greater insight into Montaigne as a conversationalist than what he says when he is ostensibly describing his public character. He tells us how he felt about the weather, about his height, his sexual prowess, children, old age; how concerned or unconcerned he was with financial matters; what he was like when he was angry, and how much wine he drank. It would be repetitious to reconstruct these details here; but this self-portrait does pose several critical problems.

First, Montaigne at times seems to lack discrimination; he describes not only how he thinks but also, for instance, how he cleans his teeth. Some readers are impatient with what seems a predilection for trivia, but if we can grasp why he talks about cleaning his teeth, we are near to understanding his mind and his sense of values. Also, the tone of these self-portrayals varies considerably. Usually Montaigne is calm and almost contemplative; elsewhere, for instance in III, ix, when he asserts his desire to be self-sufficient, he is surprisingly violent and fervent. These differences should be noted; the fervour suggests a hard-won battle, or else a matter in which he considers himself significantly different from most other men. The major problem is that some of the details of this portrait are clearly untrue. Montaigne constantly says he has a very poor memory and can retain nothing—in a book which is full of quotations and reminiscences from his reading, of anecdotes he had heard in the past or experiences which he recalls vividly. His marginal comments on his copy of Caesar prove that either he remembered other authors while reading Caesar, or remembered Caesar while reading other authors. He did, it is clear, have trouble with proper names; but these are the only lapses for which there is any evidence. In the same way, he accuses himself of laziness, but his productive life as writer, scholar and statesman hardly suggests sloth. But to deal with these problems, we must look at what Montaigne concluded about the problem of how, and how much, a man can know himself.

Works which claim to tell all have been common since the Romantic period and range in value from Rousseau and Gide to the ghost-written revelations of many an actress or even worse. So accustomed are we to this sort of literature that we are apt to forget that, in Montaigne's time, his effort was quite a novel one. He certainly considered it such, for he terms it original, trail-blazing, and even fantastic. Everyone else looks ahead or outside himself, whereas he looks inside himself; heretofore 'nemo in sese tentat descendere', he proudly claims in II, xvii. Indeed, he is not comparable to Petrarch, whose autobiographical writing is extensively concerned with aesthetic and literary matters, and with Petrarch the man primarily in order to evaluate himself as a Christian. Nor to Benvenuto Cellini's adventurous, almost picaresque Memoirs. The *Essais* more closely resemble St. Augustine's *Confessions*, the prototype of post-classical autobiography, though the two have completely different goals; Montaigne is not writing an apology of his conversion. Nor had Montaigne read, it would seem, the *Confessions*. The man he most resembles,

Cardan, he also had not read; besides, Cardan (like Rousseau and so many others) indulges in extravagant praise or deprecation of himself and his fate. There is a debt to Plutarch, but for the techniques of biography, not for the idea of autobiography; to the Roman letter-writers, for the *Essais* contain the kinds of information found in the epistles of Cicero and others, but the *Essais* are not letters. We must conclude that he did strike out on his own. What makes his doing so all the more impressive is that his contemporaries looked upon any such project as not only peculiar but even improper. It was bad enough for a gentleman to write; it was even worse for him to write about himself. Montaigne felt called upon to apologize for doing so, Marie de Gournay added excuses, Pascal termed the whole business a 'sot projet', and even his nineteenth-century English editors were defensive about his egocentric mania. If he were famous, or if he had some particular injustice to complain about, such showing of the self would have been excusable, but neither was the case.

Then, how and why did the *Essais* become autobiographical? Any answer must be hypothetical, and the hypotheses can be grouped in three categories: general, unspecific influences; the evolution of the *Essais* themselves; and certain impelling philosophical beliefs. In the first we must include not only the Latin epistolary tradition, but also Christianity, which asserts the importance of the concrete individual and is usually considered a major force in the growth of autobiography. Catholicism added the impetus of the confession, and Montaigne once compares his project to the public, non-auricular confession Protestants were demanding. But again, the *Essais* are not primarily concerned with detailing Montaigne's sins and vices. In its way, the translation of Raymond of Sebonde may have put him on the track; Sebonde felt that introspection could lead to an awareness of the divinity, the way the study of nature could. But Montaigne never seeks in his self-analysis any contemplation of God the Creator of Montaigne. More important would seem the Renaissance emphasis on individualism and heroism. Montaigne lacked the sanguine enthusiasm Burckhardt saw as characteristic of the period, but he did strongly feel that each individual mattered as an individual. So far as the Renaissance substitutes the particular for the type, Michelangelo's pietà for *the* pietà, the autobiographical evolution of the *Essais* is not astounding.

For it is a matter of an evolution towards autobiography. B is more autobiographical than A, C than B—in part, perhaps, because the success of the *Essais* made Montaigne feel free to give way to his autobiographical penchant; his public was interested, not annoyed. Indeed, Villey has traced how the *Essais* began as a compilation of quotations from others;

then Montaigne added his own reactions to those quotations, then anecdotal and autobiographical information to support his reactions, and finally, shortly before A was published, decided that portraying himself should be one of the major purposes of the book. Soon this became his central purpose.

The evolution is natural enough, but in II, viii, he suggests that the decision to be autobiographical occurred at a certain moment, when he was feeling especially melancholy (and not exuberant, as viewing his autobiography as a sign of Renaissance self-confidence would lead us to expect), and concluded that the self had to be both matter and subject of the book. He wrote autobiography not because he wanted to, nor because the sentence-form of the *Essais* lent itself naturally to subjective interpretations and reminiscences, but because he had reached the conclusion that he could only talk validly about himself. Analogies with portrait-painting made the project seem possible (though the analogy was a bad one, because a portrait is immobile whereas Montaigne remained always fascinated by change and fluctuation), and certain conclusions about the nature of knowledge made the project inevitable. In short, Montaigne's doubts about the scholastic method and the possibility of many forms of knowledge made him decide you could only judge the individual. Each man is unique, and can only be known in himself and by himself. Public reputation or fame are haphazard and usually determined by meaningless exterior appearances. You alone can know your self, and your self is the only thing you can know with certainty. His quest for knowledge led him inevitably to autobiography.

So, he concludes, everyone else looks in front of himself whereas I look inside myself, and this he did with rare and intense concentration. But there remain many problems about how to know your self and what that self may be. Some of these difficulties Montaigne only touches on casually; others he discusses almost systematically, particularly in III, ii, which is a milestone in the 'theory of autobiography'. There, his pride in what he has accomplished is matched by despair at ever pin-pointing himself. He states that the more he studies himself, the less he understands and the more he is astonished; only by chance can he on occasion manage even a partial definition of his being. The simple can state who they are, but his complexity betrays any such effort. He almost concludes, with Stendhal, that he cannot know who he is. Montaigne never experienced any crisis of self-discovery; there is no moment of intense vision into himself. On the other hand, the *Essais* are not a diary; self-knowledge was not to be gained by a day-by-day description of what he thought and did. He plunges below any such surface order, but in plunging usually only discovers a limitless chaos. In that chaos, he found some regions particularly obscure—the world of sleep and dreams, of fainting, of the unconscious. He was impatient enough with this obscurity to have himself awakened in the middle of the night, so that he might find out what sleep was like! In the *Apologie*, he extends his doubt to all forms of self-knowledge, physical as well as psychological. This is tied in with the *branle*; the self is changeable, in constant flux, and cannot be identified. Then there are the problems raised by man's double nature; we believe something and yet do not believe it, hold to something and yet condemn it. The same muscles serve for tears and laughter; vice bears the semblance of virtue. Montaigne's habitually antithetical thought placed obstacles before his self-knowledge. The particular problem of knowing the self reflected the general problem of knowing anything whatsoever.

There is also the matter of determinism. Montaigne thought he was opposed to robbery because he was a Gascon, that not only our complexion and our height but even our *facultés de l'âme*—whether or not, for instance, we are superstitious—depend on the climate and region in which we are born. But he did not conclude that from a study of what determines us we can know ourselves; his determinism is aimed not at aiding self-knowledge but at attacking our independence and our freedom.

The problem of self-knowledge is also connected, in his mind, with the problem of old age. On the one hand, as he grew older he felt freer to talk about himself (his venerability will prevent others from criticizing him); however, Montaigne also felt that his advancing years destroyed his consistency as an individual. At forty he was not what he was at twenty or thirty. The model was mobile, and the painter participated in the mobility of the model. In a diary this would pose no problem, for the change could be reflected; but Montaigne's *Essais* are not chronologically ordered. His sense of change docs lead him to attach great importance to catching his spontaneous reactions, more revealing than generalizations; and he is therefore willing to draw a contradictory portrait. His concern with flux and his acceptance of contradiction should make us beware of any too synthetic an analysis of the *Essais*. Montaigne felt that you could not be both consistent and honest.

Somewhat in contradiction to this desire to catch the spontaneous and particular is Montaigne's thesis that self-study is valid because each individual contains within himself 'la forme entière de l'humaine condition', that a study of the individual can lead to knowledge about humanity in general. The phrase has perhaps been overworked, for his immediate point in III, ii, is only that his life, while not illustrious, is still of interest because the problems of moral philosophy appear among the humble as well as among the great. He goes on to justify his worth by claiming that he presents concrete details known only to himself! But does he run the risk of seeking a sort of universality which would create a Protean, all-inclusive image? The answer is no, for anyone who has read Montaigne knows who he was, has a clear and distinct impression of the man. But to see how he avoids becoming Protean, we must look at his art and his style.

Montaigne does not try to blacken the picture of himself he draws. His desire for completeness leads him to include good and bad, but he is never apologetic, nor does he really confess any intimate sins. This rather distinctive trait (for an autobiography is usually a defence or an attack on its writer) stems in part from his universal tolerance. He tries not to criticize others and not to criticize himself. If he recounts his faults, he does so in order to assure us of his honesty and humanity, and not to indulge in self-pity. Perhaps he gave himself away when he explained that with children, even if he could make himself feared, he would still rather make himself loved; this desire to be loved is a motive in his self-portrayal.

His effort at self-knowledge presents one further problem. 'Je n'ai pas plus fait mon livre que mon livre m'a fait', he announces in II, xviii, in a C text echoed in III, ii, where he suggests that self-knowledge reveals a master form by which man can measure the validity of what he does and correct his conduct. The *Essais* served to combat his supposed laziness; words such as *ordre*, *règle* and *régler* recur frequently when he discusses them. One might say that his despair about knowing himself gave rise to a desire to create himself. Introspection then serves a therapeutic purpose; man reforms himself by self-study. Léon Brunschvicq saw in this tension between self-knowledge as confession and as self-improvement the element which makes the *Essais* a decisive event in history. Georges Gusdorf, whose book *Découverte de soi* offers a perspicacious analysis of the problems of autobiography, would agree that the genre is honest once it realizes that it is involved with becoming something, rather than with simply showing something. But before we make Montaigne a thorough existentialist, we should try to understand where and when he thinks reforming himself or the world possible, or indeed worthwhile. Because of his notion of the *branle*, he is convinced man does change, and so his book, consubstantial (his word) with him, changes also. Their relation is symbiotic, but not necessarily pedagogic. He was violently opposed to affectation and lying, and self-knowledge could help avoid these, but he did not use the *Essais* to create some ideal picture of himself to which he ought to conform.

The preponderance of the evidence points to his preoccupation with
the concrete particular, created by his despair about the possibility of
abstract, general knowledge. Montaigne was Montaigne, a certain individual who lived in a given time and place, read certain books, and
thought about certain problems. If there is a tension in the Renaissance
between universality and individuality, Montaigne is definitely on the
side of individuality. His fascination lies in his insistence that we accept
him as a distinct phenomenon, existing in history, who did not think
exactly as we do, and whom we read the way he interviewed his cannibals, not to discover ourselves but to discover how different others can
be from us.

Le branle

Montaigne was fond of motion. He dictated his *Essais* while walking about the room, thought while riding on horseback, and enjoyed
travelling. In boats, he knew motion sickness, but otherwise movement
of all sorts seems to have had a particular appeal for him. Indeed, he
travelled for the sake of travelling, without any fixed goal, and liked to
go as far and as long as possible. This fondness for motion is linked to his
sensitivity towards change; Montaigne sees man, and the whole world,
as constantly changing. His attitude towards that change—whether it is
good or bad—varies. He is grateful that unfortunate emotions are not
lasting and can be dissolved or dissipated through change. But primarily
his 'Que sçay-je', his scepticism and refusal to take any position, all stem
from his awareness of the *branle*, the changing nature of the world. This
branle provides the culminating argument of the *Apologie de Raimond
Sebond*, which takes up two-fifths of Book II. Montaigne begins by
asserting that while it is true that faith alone can grasp the mysteries of
religion, man should try to adapt his natural intellectual gifts to the ser-
vice of his beliefs. On the other hand, reason cannot be used to attack
religion; if reason's arguments in support of religion (which Sebonde had
analysed) are finally insufficient, then that reason is certainly incapable of
providing a basis for anything else. (We discuss the religious problems
raised by the *Apologie* below.) Thereupon, Montaigne begins his great
attack on human vanity, reason and knowledge. First, he proves that man
is not superior to animals; then, that learning destroys our happiness,
turns us away from honesty and from moral conduct, and that despite
human pride learning has never established anything as absolutely true.
This is because reason, the instrument of learning, is full of contradictions
and is incapable of determining any moral laws. Also the senses, which
provide reason with its information, are unreliable. Finally, the *Apologie*

concludes with a justly famous passage on the *branle*, which caps off all the other arguments. There is no constant existence, either for man or for objects; we, our judgment, all mortal things 'vont coulant et roulant sans cesse'. Nothing can ever be established, for both judge and judged are 'en continuelle mutation et branle'. The idea is developed in a borrowing from Plutarch, which Pascal was later to repeat in even more violent terms. Man is always moving from birth to death, and to try to seize life is like trying to seize water; the reason can know nothing, for everything is either about to be or has just been. No man has ever entered the same river twice, and only God, who is eternal, escapes from the flux. The idea is strikingly extended to the whole of nature at the beginning of III, ii: 'Le monde n'est qu'une branloire perenne. Toutes choses y branlent sans cesse: la terre, les rochers du Caucase, les pyramides d'Ægypte, et du branle public et du leur.' Montaigne's consciousness of change was such that even mountains and pyramids were seen as in motion.

Nor was this constant motion limited to the earth; Montaigne knew that it characterized the heavenly bodies also. Sometimes he considered the celestial movement a matter of indifference to man, who should concentrate on more pressing and realistic questions. Elsewhere, he indulged in astrology; 'le branle admirable de la voûte céleste' has power and dominion over us, and kings, monarchies, all this lowly world 'se meut au branle des moindres mouvements célestes'. This sounds like determinism, but Montaigne never felt that man could accurately describe the heavenly motions—because man himself was in motion. He refused to choose between the Copernican and the Ptolemaic system. So if he felt we should follow the celestial motions (II, xvii—seemingly a way of fulfilling our destiny), he also felt we really cannot know what they are. Montaigne thought man was unable to analyse any object scientifically (i.e. state its characteristics mathematically) because of universal motion—both viewer and viewed were changing, so nothing could ever be grasped definitively. Everything moves along in a naturally drunken state, which we, ourselves changing, cannot grasp.

This motion takes place in time, and Montaigne had a sense of history, was aware of changes in civilization, of past grandeurs which had gone. Just as he was no longer what he was in his youth, so the world was no longer what it once had been. Such change means that no law or custom possesses universal value; it also places strict temporal limits on our knowledge. Man cannot know the past or the future, but only the present; and that present is a fleeting thing, constantly becoming past. We have mentioned the problems this created in his self-knowledge; it also raised similar difficulties in science, in history, in politics and religion, made dogmatism impossible and scepticism obligatory.

It would seem, then, that Montaigne could have concluded that we should, indeed must, change with time and history. But in politics and religion he was a conservative, opposed to all forms of change. His scepticism did not lead him to seek after mobility in his own opinions. There is a significant semantic shift here; *branle* usually indicates either necessary, innate limits on what man can know, or else good qualities; in III, ix, for instance, it is the word used to describe that quality which made him so fond of travelling. *Ebranler*, on the other hand, indicates bad upheavals which should, if possible, be avoided. Anger *ébranle* our judgment, just as Luther *ébranle* the grounds of religious belief; if we trusted in God, we would not be *ébranlés* by events. *Branler* is associated with a certain regularity and inevitability of motion, *ébranler* with uncontrolled motion which shakes things to the very roots. Despite his intense awareness of flux and change, he still wanted to live in calm; he took great pride in remaining true to the faith in which he was born just as he took pride in resembling his father. To accept the existence of change and motion, to recognize the limits it puts on us, and even to enjoy it is a sign of wisdom; to precipitate it is a sign of pride and only serves to intensify our natural imperfection.

Here again we must remember that Montaigne is responding to a world which had lost any sense of the fixed and certain it might once have had. Religion had been put into doubt by the Reformation, customs by exploration, cosmography by Copernicus, the meaning of history and the practice of politics by political theory and the beginnings of philology and the science of history. That everything was in *branle* could not be doubted; but that did not offer any justification to *ébranler* everything.

Causality

This awareness of the *branle* is closely related to the problems of intention and causality. Montaigne comes close to sharing St. Paul's opinion that we do what we do not want to do, that our best intentions produce the opposite effects; if he was sure that Fortune governed the world, Fortune for him no longer possessed her medieval wheel, which at least brought down what was up and up what was down with a certain regularity. His doubts about causality cover an impressively wide range of experience. The theme occurs often in sexual matters, where will and desire do not master the body; it also comes up with itching—our hands scratch our wounds in spite of our will. He is fond of anecdotes, often comic, which illustrate the role of hazard in human affairs. One of the most amusing comes in I, xxxiv, where the painter Protogenes, tired of trying to show the froth on a dog he had been depicting, in disgust literally threw in the sponge, and got exactly the effect he had been seeking. Chance governs war; in the heat of battle, planned action is of no use and only accident determines whether ducking helps avoid a bullet or encounter one. He even thought that gunpowder would soon pass because its greater range only increased the element of chance; he was not pessimistic enough to suspect that humanity would decide helter-skelter killing was a good thing. III, x, lists many small, irrelevant causes of major political disasters. I, xlvii, concludes, in one of those soaring generalizations often found at the end of an essay, that Fortune controls not only war and exterior events but even our thoughts and our reflections; 'prudentia fallax', he appositely quotes from Manilius. Wisdom and reason are of no avail.

But what does he mean by Fortune? A partial answer is found in I, iv, where Montaigne attacks those who blame God or Fortune for disasters which befall them; he accuses them of pride in assuming that God or Fortune will hear their complaints. Fortune is then that which transcends the individual, both in his power and in his comprehension. We are not only irresolute and inconstant, he points out in II, i; we are also determined by and subjected to a great variety of influences. We are small clods of earth, of uncertain shape and texture, and cannot hope to understand how we fit into the greater scheme of things. What we cannot control or understand is labelled Fortune. The concept of Fortune then serves to humble man, and recognizing Fortune's role is a way of acquiring wisdom and tolerance. As he says in III, viii, 'C'est imprudence que d'estimer que l'humaine prudence puisse remplir le rolle de la fortune.' In Book III, he discusses at length the moral implications of his convictions about Fortune, and arrives at the 'sagesse pratique' for which he is justly famous. III, x, opens with a statement on how man must be indifferent to the vicissitudes of this world which he cannot control. We should be judged by our intentions, not by the effect of our actions which depends on chance. Also, chance may reshape our destiny at any moment, so no life should be judged successful or a failure until death; almost Aristotelian reversals are always apt to occur. In ix, Montaigne shows an intense desire for independence; he wants to owe thanks to no one, be dependent on no one. Because Fortune is haphazard, you can rely only on yourself. Throughout III, ii, he emphasizes the importance of being concerned with interior virtue rather than exterior glory. In sum, his doubts about causality made 'self-reliance', in the fullest sense, central to all his moral thinking. He even rejects the advice of doctors, 'ayant accoustumé de luicter les deffauts qui sont en moy et les dompter par moymesme' (III, vi).

Fortune might be termed necessity, good or bad luck, or the undefinable in life, and comes close to possessing the same meaning and implications as the *branle*. But Fortune often has the added notion that the contrary of what we expect or desire takes place, that if we resort to medicine to cure ourselves we become sicker, that if we study too much we become stupid; in other words, it provides a transition between the notion of the *branle* and Montaigne's predilection for the antithesis, his assertion that opposites are similar or even identical.

Antithesis

I, liv, is entitled *Des vaines subtilités*; after a first paragraph which attacks various intellectual games such as writing poems whose every line begins with the same letter, Montaigne recounts such a game he himself had indulged in which seems not vain but highly significant. He and some friends had tried to think of as many things as they could which held together by their two extremes—Sire, for instance, was a title used for king and for traders, but not for those in between; ladies of quality and of low rank were called Dames, those in between Demoiselles. Dice are used at table only by princes and in taverns; the Romans donned the same clothes for mourning and for feast days. The chapter goes on with many more examples. Bravery and fear both make us tremble. Wisdom and stupidity have the same effect when we face tribulations, for the wise govern misfortune and the stupid ignore it. 'Ceux-ci sont, par manière de dire, au deçà des accedans, les autres au delà.' Montaigne continues with other examples, but let us see what sort of thinking is going on here. This is a spatial way of conceiving things. The ignorant are at one end of the scale, the wise at the other, and in between lie suffering and misfortune; the ignorant are below suffering, the wise above, so both are untouched by it. Montaigne often thinks in this way. For instance, in the same chapter he suggests that popular, purely natural poetry is comparable to perfect artful poetry, but 'la poésie médiocre qui s'arrête entre deux, est dédaignée, sans honneur et sans prix'. There are two opposite extremes, popular poetry and artful poetry; the former is above, the latter below what is in between—mediocre poetry. The basic idea is that opposite extremes possess certain common qualities. In III this leads him to some very 'modern' remarks about the resemblances between *douleur* and *volupté*. These opposite qualities may be bad ones as well as good; indeed, Montaigne's campaign for moderation is based on the argument that either extreme is bad because the one possesses the same defects as the other. Excessive ardour produces the same incapacity in love as lack of any ardour. I, xxx, on moderation, is full of such examples. Here we also find a slightly different thesis: an excess in a good quality produces its opposite. Again, Montaigne offers a spatial example—the archer who shoots beyond the goal is as amiss as the one who does not get to it. 'On peut et trop aimer la vertu, et se porter excessivement en une action juste.' The principle is immediately applied to marriage, where too much affection ruins domestic calm. An excess of otherwise good humours produces bad health. Moderation is needed in all virtues.

There are two sub-classes of this way of thinking in Montaigne. One is the idea that an individual who is excessively good at something is also no good at it; the extremely learned are ignorant, the doctor is often ill (the most frequent example), the theologian immoral, the shoemaker badly shod. Excess again produces an absence of the qualities sought after, but here the problem is located in one person. Another less frequent but related notion is that excess is apparent in opposite values. This is harder to describe graphically—the notion is that if someone is extreme, his intensity is manifest at two poles. The Romans were a powerful, energetic people, who surpassed us in virtue and, as well, in vice. The obverse of this is that diametrically opposed traits really stem from a common cause; avarice and prodigality, for instance, both show an undue preoccupation with material goods. Montaigne extends this parallel of extremes with great facility. I, xxxviii, is entitled *Comme nous pleurons et rions d'une même chose*, and lists instances where the same cause produces these opposite effects. The theme carries over to assertions such as we find in II, xxxv—women who laugh with their husbands during life may weep at their death, but wives who have been tearful should start laughing once they are widowed. Here the laughter–tears similarity has been applied to a lived situation where an element of time enters in; it is often such a lapse of time which makes the opposites become equals.

We might try to categorize these antitheses. The extremes can be labelled *a* and *z* (learning and stupidity, laughter and tears, etc.). When Montaigne thinks of *a*, he thinks of *z*. He sees man as caught between the two, for instance by hunger and thirst, with ham on one side and beer on the other (the image is his). *A* and *z* produce the same result. *A* and *z* may stem from the same cause. An excess of *a* may produce *z*; or *a* and *z* both avoid the dangers of the middle. Or *a* and *z* are both to be avoided in favour of the middle term—moderation is needed in all virtues. These forms of thought are closely related, and Montaigne moves with ease from one to another. Often, he considers extremes equally vicious, and the fact that they have much in common proves that they ought to be avoided. At other times, he suggests that one extreme be used to meet and combat another; if we reversed things, and made the poor wear expensive clothes, the demand for such luxuries would soon decrease. Occasionally, he finds consolation in the equivalence of these extremes; bad passions can be the source of good actions. Or he favours some kind of blending and reconciliation—pure virtues cannot serve without 'composition', just as certain metals must be blended with an alloy to be of use. But more often he concludes either that man should avoid any and all excesses—of vice, but also of virtue—or else that the equivalence of opposites is a ground for pessimism. For this way of thinking is clearly related to Montaigne's preoccupation with the vagaries of causality; two diametrically opposed means may produce the same effect, or the same means produce two completely different effects. To say that in civil war attempts to defend yourself assure that you will be attacked is a way of saying not only that intentions are betrayed by circumstances, but also that the opposites defence–attack are equivalents.

Where this antithetical way of thinking comes from remains hypothetical. It is an aspect of the Socratic method, and indeed of Thomism—Aquinas' *sed contra* prepares for Montaigne. Probably the formulas were acquired at school. But the bent to see things as opposites seems to have been a deep, natural and pervasive one. Stylistically, it gives rise to sentences which are balanced in two parts, to paradoxes and even chiasmus. Whole chapters are antithetically organized—the chapter on suicide gives the arguments for, and then the arguments against. And within any chapter, thought after thought falls into one of the antithetical patterns. But this is perhaps only the most evident of Montaigne's mental mechanisms; a careful reading to discover some of the others would be fruitful.

Nature

In our introduction, we mentioned the language problems encountered in reading Montaigne. The most difficult is that presented by those words which are important in expressing his thought and yet have a sense for him which does not include some of the meanings we give them and does include other meanings we usually do not give them. This is true of any author, so far as that author reshapes a language to his own use; so trying to find out what Corneille meant by *gloire* or Mallarmé by *désastre* is a very good way of discovering what the author has to say. With Montaigne, the words *nature*, *naturel* provide an excellent and important illustration. Let us construct a few sentences in which we would use them today. 'Two-headed children are monstrous, they are not natural; they are luckily very rare indeed.' 'The law of gravity is a natural law.' 'When the house caught on fire, instead of using her head she did the natural thing, grabbed her teakettle, and ran as fast as she could.' 'He is a very affected young man and speaks in an artificial, rather than a natural way.' Of these four sentences, Montaigne could only have written the last; his notion of what is natural does not encompass the usage involved in the first three. Once we grasp this, we can understand what he means when he says that virtue should be natural.

Let us take the first sentence. Montaigne always distinguishes between what is not customary and what is not natural. A monstrous child was born by a natural process, so though it may be unusual or even unpleasant, it is part of God's creation and hence natural. Cannibalism may have its disadvantages as well as its advantages, but since in certain societies it is unquestioned, it is natural. In Montaigne's eyes, anything which is, is part of the infinite complexity of nature; the rare and the exceptional—be they earthquakes or Siamese twins—are not unnatural. Perhaps more difficult for us to see is why he would not call the law of gravity natural. For Montaigne, the universe is infinitely complex and undefinable, and any statement about it is therefore a falsification. Such a statement is imposed on nature, and hence unnatural; he compares such laws to false teeth and face powder. Hiram Haydn, in his excellent book on the Counter-Renaissance, sees in Montaigne an advocate of 'natural humanism', that is, someone 'who thought of nature as something quite different from reason'. This is not entirely accurate; Montaigne rather considers that reason and instinct are one and the same thing, and may both be labelled natural. In the *Apologie* he makes a great point of refusing to distinguish between the behaviour of animals and the behaviour of men, between instinct and reason. His cat may be playing with him, not he with the cat. So Montaigne would never speak of instinctive conduct as being unnatural; he would reserve that label for unreasonable conduct and say of our lady with the teapot that she did the unnatural thing instead of reasonably, instinctively and naturally grabbing her mink coat.

Montaigne would accept such uses as 'natural aptitude,' 'natural vocation'. Men differ; cripples are not good runners, etc.; each has his own nature and there is a role in life befitting that nature. He admired Plato for exploiting this notion in the *Republic*. His distinction between repentance and regret, in III, ii, reflects this notion of being true to your nature. You may regret that your nature is what it is, but you can only repent about matters which are changeable, which are not part of your character. Montaigne, for instance, could manage to be a satisfactory mayor but it was not natural for him; his virtues there were difficult and artificial.

This brings us to the key distinction—the sentence he could write, which distinguishes between the natural and the artificial. For Montaigne the natural is good, the artificial is bad. This shows first in his praise of himself; if he is honest and sincere, it is because 'je me laisse aller après ma nature, à faute d'art'. Many of his anti-medical remarks are justified in these terms. He refuses to consult doctors and instead 'laisse faire nature', assuming that nature has the means to defend itself, that the unaided body can resist any attack. These two notions (nature equals sincerity, nature can take care of itself) seem close to Rousseau's claim that nature is in itself good; but the emphasis is completely different. The correct way to put it would be to say that artifice is not completely bad, but rather is inadequate and perverts the purpose it is intended to serve— which brings us back to the problem of causality. Medicines do not cure people; they only make them more ill. Artifice is connected with the arts —the knowing how—and man simply does not know how. Nature has of itself a kind of purity and beauty for which the practice of art substitutes something he at one point calls horror.

But if, when Montaigne speaks of Nature in opposition to artifice, Nature is good, when he speaks of Nature without the contrast of artifice, especially of his own nature, he is less convinced of its excellence. Take his remarks on clothing. At times he suggests that clothing is dishonest and misleading; it hides our true character and our actual physical state. He also feels that the use of clothing has destroyed our natural capacity to protect ourselves. Animals do without clothing, as man once could but no longer can; so here again artifice has vitiated our nature. But elsewhere he suggests that man—or woman—in the nude is an ugly thing indeed, and that we are well advised to cover ourselves. He was not completely satisfied with his own nature by any means, and when he was unhappy in love accused Nature of having done a bad job by him.

So Montaigne does not always claim that Nature is entirely good, and is willing to admit that the practice of artifice may on occasion be advisable. But the evolutionary thought involved in his suggestion that wearing clothing has changed man's nature allows him to conclude that artifice is all right if it is practised long enough to become natural. II, xi, develops this notion that virtue can become a part of our complexion, the very essence of our soul, and then be easy and natural. The unnatural is not what you do after reasoning, it is only what you do which is difficult and dishonest. It is all right to choose a certain virtuous form of conduct, as long as you discipline yourself to the point of doing it naturally and easily. For if you do it with your reason alone, you will not succeed; you will only become involved in a web of contradictions. Socrates offers the ideal of someone who practised discipline to the point where virtue became easy and natural for him. But clearly one can practise a discipline which will make vice easy and natural—the weaknesses induced by wearing clothing are a case in point. In short, natural conduct may be either good or bad; artificial conduct is inefficacious, and therefore bad. *Vertu* should always be *naturelle*, but *nature* is not necessarily *vertueuse*.

Death

Death is one of the most frequent subjects of the *Essais*, and is also one on which Montaigne seems most contradictory. I, xx, by its title informs us that to philosophize is to learn how to die, and maintains that the goal of virtue is to make us indifferent to death. Death is inevitable; not to think of it is a vulgar and stupid remedy. We may die at any moment of the slightest cause; rather than be surprised, we should expect death everywhere. If we can conquer our fear of death, we can face all the tribulations of life with equanimity. We die a bit every day, and must seek consolation, seemingly in such syllogisms as if we do not regret not living a hundred years ago, why regret not living a hundred years from now? or, a quick death gives us little time for regrets, whereas a long illness takes away our desire to live, so either diminishes the impact of death.

Many of these thoughts come from classical literature, often from Stoic sources. One sometimes feels that Montaigne is grasping the straws of classic sophistry in a strenuous effort to embolden himself for the crisis. Christian thoughts on death as a deliverance from the sorrows of this life, on the immortality of the soul, are absent; nor does he reflect any Platonic ideas about immortality—only the Renaissance notion that a difficult death can be a means of glory. There are occasional strains of the Renaissance version of the dance of death theme: the life of a triumphant emperor is the lunch of a small worm, death renders all life meaningless. But we should not conclude that these ideas are only collected from literary sources, for we find them in one of the most sincere and moving pieces of prose Montaigne wrote, his 1563 letter to his father about the death of La Boétie. La Boétie died a true Stoic, and Montaigne admired his 'brave démarche', his 'courage invincible' in front of pain and death. He refused all distractions, and his last words were: 'let her come when she will, I'm waiting, brave and firm footed, for "An vivere tanti est?"'; he remained conscious and intelligent through his three days of agony to the very end. The death of this idolized friend certainly left its mark on Montaigne, and a desire to have an equally good death creates much of the tension in I, xx, and other early thoughts on mortality.

But in B and C we encounter a quite different tone and arguments of a very different sort. In III, ix, he asserts that he would prefer to die alone, with a minimum of attentions and ceremonies, as unostentatiously and as easily as possible, and he recounts dreams of various voluptuous sorts of deaths. III, xii, goes even further. During the plague, Montaigne was struck by the example of the poor who met death quietly and with equanimity, bravely digging their own graves; they naturally knew how to die. He concludes that we should not prepare for misfortunes, but accept them as they come; preparing for death has caused more trouble and sorrow than the actual physical suffering. Death is not the goal of life, only its end, and we should be concerned with knowing how to live, not with how to die. All the emphasis is on seeing in death a normal part of man's fate; the message is, the less fuss the better—whereas earlier Montaigne seemingly sought in death an occasion for displaying heroic strength.

But in I, xx, Montaigne is also seeking after tranquillity; *volupté* is the goal of his virtue, and he wants to die while planting his cabbages, to accept death as something necessary and natural. If changes took place in his thought, it was not that he differed about how to die, but about how to prepare to die in that way—as painlessly and as unostentatiously as possible. Where he varies is that in the earlier essays he thinks the more preparation the better, whereas he later decides that preparation is futile; man will naturally know what to do when death comes. In a sense, Montaigne has become more optimistic about man; he will know how to die naturally. In another sense, he has become more pessimistic; thinking about and preparing for death is vain. In any case, he has become more personal; the later essays owe more to what he has seen, and less to what he has read, just as they are more concerned with his death, and less concerned with death in general. Montaigne's *Essais* did indeed form him, and by the time he came to write the later ones, he had learned to accept death, or at least had so re-evaluated life that death no longer seemed such a shocking event; thus accepting it as natural became a good deal easier. Once he had put life in its proper perspective, he could maintain that death was natural for him and should be natural for others. We cannot say that he turned his back on death; on the contrary, he moved from an abstract concern to an immediate, personal concern. He tried to make what at first seemed unique and exceptional into something which would be fully a part of man's fate and accepted as such. Nor is he, in the *Essais*, concerned with any thoughts about death which transcend the conditions of human life—such as immortality. A discussion of such transcendent concerns would strike him as irrelevant to the book. And he seems himself, from what Pasquier and Pierre de Brach tell us, to have died well.

Religion

Montaigne was always afraid that he might be misunderstood, and as far as religious beliefs go we must conclude that he has been. Generally, Protestants have claimed he was really a Protestant, agnostics that he was an agnostic disguised as an indifferent Catholic in order to avoid persecution, Catholics that he was a devout though perhaps peculiar Catholic. The more we know about Montaigne, the more apparent it is that he was a devout Catholic; the more we know about history, the more we see that he was really not such a peculiar Catholic.

The evidence from his life is clear. He had mass said daily in his château, even when his neighbourhood was in Protestant hands. When travelling, he heard mass regularly, visited shrines, made votive offerings. Upon dying, he received the rites of the Church. He was quick to take any oath of religious loyalty. And his practice of the faith extended beyond liturgical worship. He defended the *pater* as superior to all other prayers, and he used the sign of the cross sparingly because he was especially devoted to it. These details belie the picture of a man playing at Catholicism; instead, they suggest someone who lived his religion. In later ages, such ostensible Catholicism could be either a sign of political opportunism or else demonstrate a public support of the Church as an institution 'good for the people' but in which you yourself did not fully believe. But Montaigne never defends the Church as a valuable social institution, though he does attack Protestantism as socially pernicious. Nor was his Catholicism the product of political opportunism. He was not politically ambitious, and he could perfectly well have been a Protestant if he had wanted to; most of his important neighbours were, as was the rising political star, his friend Henri of Navarre. If Montaigne had been a Protestant, he might have suffered for his beliefs, but he was equally likely to suffer for his Catholicism, and his open insistence on the practice of his faith was a sign of courage.

Montaigne rejected Protestantism for a number of other reasons. He felt Protestants were presumptuous. Their confidence in their ability to interpret the Bible struck him as the height of human pride; he is extremely sarcastic in his portrait of cooks and valets with greasy fingers leafing through Holy Writ. The Protestants had created civil discord and strife, again because of their self-righteousness and intellectual pride.

There was nothing nominal about sixteenth-century Protestantism; it demanded total adherence to a system of theology and a series of beliefs. If we reconstruct Protestantism before nineteenth-century liberalism left its mark, and Catholicism before the Council of Trent had defined so many matters of doctrine, we see why someone like Montaigne, who wished to preserve a maximum of intellectual liberty and remain as un-categorical as possible, would feel more at ease as a Catholic than as a Calvinist or Lutheran. Catholicism offered that combination of per-manence and elasticity he prized above all else.

But did he relegate religion to one compartment of his life, and in others pursue a course of free intellectual inquiry which led to con-clusions which could not be reconciled with his religious belief? This interpretation of Montaigne's Catholicism as rather schizophrenic has often been convincingly advanced, but there is some important evidence against it. For instance, it is asked how can Montaigne have been a serious Catholic when he advocates suicide? But he does not really advo-cate suicide; he admires certain suicides as manifestations of the heroism of classical antiquity, he is fascinated with suicide as part of the problem of how to die and what meaning to give death, and he weighs the pros and cons of suicide as carefully as he weighs the pros and cons of every-thing. Among the pros, he does place St. Paul's willingness to die for Christ, which may astound us, but we must remember that suicide was not then formally condemned by the Church with the vigour with which it is condemned today.

The second problem is that Montaigne seems a fideist; that is, he be-lieves the reason is of no avail in proving the verities of the Church, which must be accepted by an act of faith alone; this act of faith, except so far as it is determined by the accident of when and where we were born, is purely gratuitous. The *Apologie* elaborates the fideist thesis, which is all the more surprising since Sebonde's basic argument was that human reason could perceive proofs of the existence of God, etc., in creation; Montaigne denies that the reason has any such power. He was evidently unaware of the distinction between natural truths which the unaided reason can discover (e.g. the existence of an omnipotent God the creator) and the revealed truths (the Incarnation, the Atonement, the Trinity) which can only be known through Grace. In the *Apologie*, he attacks those who, with the reason, question revealed truths—in parti-cular, the Reformed theologians. He extends his critique a great deal further, but not in order to attack the Catholic faith; he leaves the re-ligious context behind, and attacks human reason and pride. Elsewhere, he almost defends the theory of natural revelation, the notion that we find in primitive cultures which cannot have known Christ, such Christian traits as the cross and the celibate priesthood; he comes close to maintaining that the Christian religion can be proved by analogy. Secondly, the traditional fideist approach, maintained in the Renaissance by the Paduan school, is quite different from that of II, xii. The fideists claimed that by faith they knew *a* (the doctrine of the Church) to be true, by reason they knew *b* (something which could well be in contradiction with the doctrine of the Church) to be true. Montaigne claims that by faith he knows *a* to be true, whereas by reason there is nothing he knows to be true. The whole purpose of the *Apologie* is to prove, not that reason contradicts faith, but that reason cannot contradict faith—because reason, which is self-contradictory, cannot prove or disprove anything.

The *Apologie* does raise another question. There is a tradition of Christian writing which tries to induce humility and indicate the smallness of man in comparison to the glory of God; but this tradition emphasizes man's mortality, his corruptibility, his incapacity to conquer himself without the help of God, his thoroughly evil nature. Montaigne's attack on man is made in quite different terms and in a quite different tone; you need only think of the Imitation of Thomas à Kempis to realize how different. Montaigne abandons the Christian tradition of showing the hopeless state of man in his need for grace. The attacks on the contradictions of science found in II, xii, for an example, are not found in medieval apologetics. III, ix, is entitled *De la vanité* but is largely concerned with the impossibility of being virtuous; man must know his limits, not by comparing himself to God, but by realizing how he cannot do what he wants to do in a corrupt and unreliable world. We partake of this corruption, and all men merit hanging at least ten times; but if Montaigne wants us to recognize this, it is only in order to destroy our self-righteousness and our optimism which lead to a zeal he thought nefarious. Montaigne may attack pride and vainglory, but the language and purpose of his attack are novel. This becomes understandable when we remember that the enemy was different. Montaigne is writing at the end of the Renaissance; the exuberance and self-confidence he is attacking are not the pride Thomas à Kempis was dealing with.

There remains the more difficult problem of the almost total absence of Christian concerns, which certainly suggests indifference, in page after page of the *Essais*. The disquieting thing about the chapter on suicide is not that he defends suicide, nor that his two quotations from the Bible are in favour of it, but that he never discusses it from what could be termed a Christian perspective. We are tempted to conclude that if Montaigne was not a theoretical fideist, he was a practical one, who kept his religious experience in one compartment of his life. There are only some three dozen quotations from the Bible (including those on the walls), and these, mostly from Paul and the Wisdom literature, deal with human weakness. What is surprising is not that he should admire Julian the Apostate, even if the Church censors objected, but that all the men he admires are either heroes of pagan antiquity or else 'cannibals'—primitives. When he indulges in an apologetic note, to claim for instance that man needs images in order to worship or that man is moved by the architecture of churches, he is not writing any Renaissance *Génie du christianisme* but simply showing what human nature is, what its needs and responses are; the religious context is accidental. But Montaigne makes a sharp distinction between humanists and theologians; theologians are a group apart, and he was (because of the Reformation) violently opposed to any amateur ventures in that domain, including any he might make. He may have believed that there was a theological solution to the problems he studied, but the *Essais* examine those problems outside that theological context. Indeed, the *Apologie* maintains that since man is easily swayed by every argument, since there is no rational basis for belief, then there can be no questioning of belief. That there are no arguments in support of the faith means that there can be no arguments against it, and this in its way constitutes a defence of the faith. Thus, even if Montaigne seems a sceptic, his thought is much less radical than that of such contemporaries as Etienne Dolet or Bonaventure des Périers; he may bring everything into question, but he refuses to solve any of the questions, and so they never in any way really attack religion.

This is all the more true because Montaigne's religious thought is characterized by an awareness of the otherness of God. He is opposed to any form of anthropomorphism; man is not the image of God, but rather by his imperfection completely separate from God who is beyond human understanding. Montaigne has the Augustinian sense of the immense gulf which separates man from the Divinity. The majesty of God is manifest in the most incomprehensible aspects of the universe, and therefore belief is the highest form of our lack of knowledge, the admission of our own uncertainties and by contrast of the glory of God. But such a God is rather far away from those concerns of daily life which mark Montaigne's volume. When man tries to get close to God, Montaigne turns to him to say: 'enfle-toi, tu crèveras'; only in renouncing all preoccupation with our own being do we perceive God. This renunciation Montaigne was willing to make in principle, but not often in practice. However, there is no sign that Montaigne ever doubted the existence of God; this is why his attacks on the weakness of man never acquire tragic tones. His despair in philosophy is covered by his certitude in theology, so philosophical doubt can indeed give him a soft pillow on which to rest.

Politics

In III, i, Montaigne makes a radical distinction between public and private virtue. In private matters, it is possible to adhere to a strict moral code and never sacrifice your convictions to expediency; in public matters, no such morality is possible. The state is corrupt, so the magistrate must lie, the king be cruel and punish. Therefore the citizen should try to limit his involvement in politics. He should be loyal to his king as a citizen, but not as a partisan; he should support the good cause 'jusqu'au feu, mais exclusivement', and so far as possible take the middle road in civil strife and dissension. Once you enter the world of politics, vices such as lying become legitimate, you persecute friends and relatives for the sake of 'justice'; so Montaigne avoided political involvement and urged others to do likewise.

It is often said that Montaigne and Machiavelli—at least the Machiavelli of the common image—agreed in their analysis of the corruption politics involved, and disagreed only in their conclusion; whereas Machiavelli recommends getting rid of moral preoccupations and practising realistic politics, Montaigne recommends getting rid of politics. The contrast is useful, but we must remember that Montaigne is addressing not a prince but a private citizen (he has his own message for princes, and it is a stringent one) and that his refusal of politics stems from his feeling that in the instance the ends do not justify the means involved; the possibilities of improving the political situation are so slim that it is best to do only what you must and otherwise wash your hands of the whole business. Montaigne's scepticism is at the root of his refusal to get politically involved. Justice and government are necessarily corrupt and inefficacious because human society is corrupt and unstable. The unreliable, changeable nature of the world makes it unwise to put any trust in princes or causes, or to sacrifice one's own sense of duty to the demands posed by being a French citizen or by being mayor of Bordeaux. Indeed, this is stating Montaigne's position rather mildly; he goes so far as the *suave maris magno* attitude: it is comfortable to dwell, morally self-satisfied, in your tower, and watch the vain turmoil and suffering about you.

Yet, in his way Montaigne provides a detailed political programme. He is very much opposed to duels; he is against the use of torture in judicial proceedings, and his criticisms of the courts for being unduly concerned with procedure or even corrupt are quite specific and detailed, even if they are commonplace. He laments the political state of France and complains about the religious wars. In the matter of duels, torture and imperialism he is well ahead of his time. His condemnation of the abuses involved in the conquest of America is impressive, though his political attitude here is influenced by his appreciation for the primitive. Yet, it should be noted that in III, vi, he admires these 'primitives' not only for their moral virtues, but also for their advanced civilization; they are noble, but they are not really savages. More important, Montaigne offers a definition of the prince in its way as detailed and as demanding as that of Machiavelli. It is regrettable that he is less often contrasted with that other Italian, Castiglione, with whom he also significantly agrees and disagrees. The courtiers of Castiglione's Urbino share Montaigne's pessimistic analysis of the outside world and the chances of making sense out of it; they, too, have retired into a sort of tower. But Montaigne's picture of the ideal nobleman almost contradicts the *Courtier* point by point. Montaigne does not want his prince to be a good dancer, or a good conversationalist, or a gourmet; indeed, he does not want him to practise any of the 'civilized arts' so highly valued in Castiglione's work. Far from proposing any ideal of Platonic love, he admires his political heroes for their sexual as well as their military conquests. Despite his pessimistic analysis of politics and of the possibility of moral behaviour in the political realm, certain heroes of the past—Alexander, Caesar, Epaminondas—rank among his favourite men, and, from his close study of their lives, he derived principles which the prince of his day could follow. These principles can be reconstructed from various essays, which include, for instance, detailed debates on whether or not the prince should accompany his soldiers to battle. Basically, he demands of the prince single-minded devotion to political efficacy. When not attacking the proud fervour of partisanship, he admits that politics is a necessary evil in which power and efficiency—heroic virtues—are the goals to be sought; in other words, he comes close to Machiavelli. He praises Alcibiades who for the sake of power was voluptuous in Ionia, austere in Sparta, just as he praises an ambassador who learned how to get drunk in order to get along with the Germans. In these instances, moral virtues are willingly sacrificed for political efficacy—in complete contradiction to what he recommends in III, i. Unambiguous praise is reserved for such as the Roman emperor Vespasian who, in the face of death and despite the counsel of his physicians, continued extending his empire, working intensely until the very end. The prince should not only avoid luxury; he should barely eat and drink, and give himself up entirely to the great, virtuous, beautiful tasks history offers him.

Can this hero-worshipping acceptance of the romance of princedom, on the one hand, and this caustic despair about and even annoyance with any signs of political fervour and conviction, on the other, be reconciled? It helps to remember that he is addressing two different publics: princes, who were obliged to take sides and act, and *l'homme moyen*, who Jean Bodin thought had to choose sides, and Justus Lipsius thought did not. Montaigne tended to agree with Lipsius; if a choice had to be made, *l'homme moyen* should make it in terms of where and when he was born, and not in terms of any convictions of his own. Nor is this Montaigne's only effort at compromise on political matters. He was opposed to large armies, because they were of little use, too difficult to feed, equip and direct; a few good men are worth a great many indifferent ones. Politics may be evil, but it is a necessary evil, and the necessity should be handed over to those best equipped to deal with it; his preference for small armies is a sign of moderation, and yet is also in line with his cult of heroism. To each of us is given a character, that character determines our political destiny, and we can be both heroic and practical only by being true to that character. Nowhere is this compromise solution more evident than in his analysis of the nature of laws. Usually, Montaigne is opposed to any change in the laws, just as he is opposed to civil disobedience. Instability in politics seemed to him the worst evil, to be avoided at any cost. Indeed, all his political thinking reflects what can only be described as his bitterness about the turbulent state of France in his age; this bitterness is particularly apparent in III, iv. Yet, the *Apologie* regards change as the one constant. Everything changes, so should not government and the laws do likewise? The answer is that the laws must be maintained, not because they are good, but because they are laws. For Montaigne, natural variation is such that there can be no good law; human behaviour is so diverse that laws cannot be formulated in terms of that behaviour. This diversity already requires that what laws there are be interpreted endlessly, the interpretations vary with the interpreters, and the result is chaos. A C text in III, ix, extends the notion that 'tout crolle autour de nous' from the physical world to the political world; in such a world, iniquity was bound to prevail. So a measure of realism which could prevent idealistic fanaticism, and a sense of measure which would at least limit the nefarious effects of change, offered the only solution; but that pessimistic solution sounds against the background of an intense opposition to cruelty in all its forms.

For Montaigne is a moralist, even in his political theory. Late Renaissance moralists, though they may propose some definition of the ultimate good, are primarily men who study mores, and such is Montaigne.

Indeed, the flourishing of political theory at the time gave new vigour to the study of mores, for people hoped to learn how to manipulate men through observing and describing them. From that study a political ethic of pure expediency was usually derived, by Machiavelli, Guicciardini, or Bodin as well as by Montaigne. Montaigne seems less pessimistic than Machiavelli only because he thinks the degree of political involvement required of a man is less; there, the difference between being a citizen of an Italian city-state and a citizen of a still largely feudal France may explain the contrast. Finally, political matters are practical matters; Montaigne may have felt it was possible to place certain questions which were the object of individual control in the ethical realm—such as the practice of cruelty—and that certain unethical procedures were also politically valueless—such as torture and lying—but he felt that 'une vertu scolastique et novice' was impossible in the world. Indeed, how to redefine virtue so that it would be possible was in a way his unique task. To be possible, it had to be easy; and the complexity and unreliability of politics prevented any ease.

PART III

The art of the 'Essais'

It is very difficult to stop in the middle of a Montaigne essay; even the *Apologie*, which constitutes about a sixth of the whole work, begs to be read from beginning to end. In this, Montaigne is quite different from Pascal; the *Pensées* make excellent bedside reading, but the *Essais* do not. The transitions may seem haphazard, but it would be more correct to term them challenging. Something has always served to lead him from one subject to the next; the more you come to understand Montaigne and to think as he does, the less these transitions astonish. In the editions published during his lifetime, there were no paragraphs; we might regret their introduction by later editors, for they destroy the organic flow at which Montaigne aimed. At times his method of organization is almost that of a modern poet, who sets side by side ideas which at first seem to be unrelated but which, when juxtaposed, cast a pertinent and revealing light on each other. For finally, Montaigne's unity stems from his desire for universality; he strives to express, in a given chapter, everything pertinent to its subject, every possible perspective. Because of this, it was perfectly natural for him to add to an essay. Time, experience, additional reading had given him new thoughts on the question of friendship; he introduces those thoughts into the essay at the points where they will best serve to give a universal picture. One of Montaigne's most competent critics, Professor Plattard, regrets the cumbersome additions of C, which he feels destroy the logical sequence and easy flow the B version of an essay possesses. You should try to find out; read, preferably from Book II, an essay while skipping over the C passages; then re-read the essay with those passages. The shorter form may seem simpler and clearer—though I suspect the problem of Montaigne's transitions remains what it is in the final version, for the same kind of thinking goes into composing the essay as goes into making the additions—but does it seem as complete and adequate as the longer one? It is only with C that Montaigne becomes convinced that his experience has universal significance, that he solves the problem of the relation between virtue and natural behaviour. Montaigne was a richer, fuller man when he made his last edition; he had conquered the problem of being Mayor; he had come to terms with the problem of pain. He was reading Cicero with care and understanding, whom he had long neglected but who perhaps had more to say about how to make your peace with this world than did either Seneca or Plutarch. For the fullness of the picture he offers us, we need these illuminations from his later years. Some authors, for the sake of form, sacrifice the richness of their thought, or at least its ambiguous complexity. Montaigne is at the opposite extreme; he insists on sacrificing an appearance of order and coherence to completeness. His closest emulator here is probably a man who did not understand him at all, as like often does not understand like, Jules Michelet. But whereas Michelet achieves completeness by multiplying adjectives, nouns and clauses, Montaigne, who is a less self-assured, less lyrical thinker, achieves it more often by adding new ideas and new perspectives. To condemn either is to prefer clarity of organization to richness of content.

Admittedly, it is hard to understand why certain essays have the title they have, and their unity is not immediately apparent. In other essays, the material may indeed seem to be all about education or suicide, but it is hard to see why Montaigne should move from point *a* to point *b*; indeed, sometimes even his quotations or his anecdotes seem impertinent to the point they supposedly illustrate. To make matters worse, there are many statements in which Montaigne agrees, often with candid indifference, that his essays are badly organized. These statements vary in tone. Some seem perfectly forthright complaints about the trouble he has composing, drawing effective conclusions, or marshalling his evidence in a telling manner. Others are so exaggerated that we wonder if they are to be taken at face value, or whether Montaigne is not criticizing himself in order to parry the criticisms of others or else as part of his general desire to humble intellectual effort. When he calls the *Essais* grotesque and monstrous, without order, sequence or proportion, we must conclude he is exaggerating. We can take seriously his claim that he does not have enough wind to manage a lengthy organization, but not when he adds that he is more ignorant than a child of the words and phrases needed to express the most common ideas. There is something of the *poseur* about these claims of incompetency. Montaigne is given to self-deprecation, and his complaints about his lack of organization must be partly discounted as manifestations of this tendency. He sometimes claims that he is disorderly because he wants to be, not because he has to be, that he is more concerned with the weight and usefulness of his *Essais* than with their order and sequence. As we shall see, he often takes pride in a certain sort of disorder, or rather in the absence of a certain kind of order. Frequently, when he admits to disorder or a sloppy transition, it is in a comic vein. In I, xlvi, he assures us that the essay will be 'une salade' of everything, and in I, xlvii, he says that since he likes to stay seated on horseback, he might just as well remain on the subject of horses. Such comic justifications of his lack of order suggest either that organization, as defined by some, was a matter of indifference to him, or else that the claims of disorder more often reflect a general tendency to attack his own worth than they do any sincere judgment of his weaknesses.

Most critics, however, have taken very seriously his assertion that he is badly organized, and there is exterior evidence to justify them. The way in which he composed the *Essais*, beginning with quotations and then commenting on them, or adding new ideas to his thoughts of several years before, would naturally lead to a badly organized, incoherent chapter where each idea in itself might be rich but the sequence of ideas haphazard. Order is something we usually impose on our ideas; we have a half-dozen thoughts on some subject and then by a rational effort decide in what way they should be presented. But Montaigne would regard such ordering as the practice of artifice which would deprive his *Essais* of any natural or sincere expression. His desire to be natural led him to seek a conversational order which moves at random from subject to subject, and where the transitions may well be fortuitous or even gratuitous. Indeed, Georges Gusdorf, in his study on the problem of self-knowledge, claims that Montaigne's effort to know himself is partly successful *because* he is disorganized and thereby manages to express the rich complexity of his life rather than imposing on it some artificial scheme which would force him to leave out large parts of what he had to say.

Such emphasis on the disorder of the *Essais* risks leading to two abuses. One is the exaggerated quest for a chronological order—to explain the contradictions of the *Essais* by the date at which Montaigne composed them. The other is a tendency to examine passages out of context, to decide that Montaigne's statements can be reshuffled into meaningful sequence while paying no heed to the arrangement he himself gave them. Everyone knows how dangerously misleading such a technique can be in political debate; it is equally dangerous in studying an author.

Other remarks by Montaigne on the problem of organization also give us pause. For one thing, when he attacks orderly organization he is often attacking what he calls rhetoric. I, li, expresses his violent antipathy to any prose which tries to persuade by false means and in I, xxvi, he maintains that the student should learn to speak the truth without the embellishments of rhetoric, its silly syllogisms, and all its rules about what should come first and how matters should be emphasized. Linkings and transitions should be hidden so that they seem natural and easy. Here, Montaigne is not only reacting against the abuses of medieval logic

Rabelais satirized; he is taking sides in the Renaissance quarrel between the admirers of Cicero, with his highly organized style and artifices of structure, and those of Seneca, with his 'amble', his flowing style and his more open, natural organization. Montaigne was entirely on the side of Seneca. But to refuse the rules, divisions and artifices of the Ciceronian structure does not mean that you are no longer concerned with grouping your thoughts in an effective way. Many remarks in the *Essais* indicate just the contrary. Montaigne often announces that he is not pursuing a development further because it would lead him too far from his thesis; he prefers in II, x, those authors who fly steadily to their goal (Virgil) to those who leap and jump about (Ariosto). In conversations and discussions, the one thing he required was order. He objected to the Ciceronian style in part because its long preparations prevent getting to the heart of the matter, and its artificial order distracts from content. Montaigne then wants, not disorder, but what he considers a better, more organic sort of order. Finally, there is his disquieting remark that if the *Essais* seem chaotic, 'c'est l'indiligent lecteur qui perd son sujet, non pas moi'—it is we who have not taken the trouble to grasp the sequence of his thought.

There are various ways of ordering one's thoughts and ideas. In a sense, with the Cartesian emphasis on method, the Ciceronians won the battle against the Senecans. But Montaigne wanted an open form which did not sacrifice richness of meaning to oratorical effect. Therefore, if he has an apposite quotation which yet goes beyond the point he wants to make, he includes it all the same; his point will be made, and what goes beyond the point is just added riches for the reader. This bonus does not make the quotation irrelevant. Montaigne seems to imitate the structure of Ovid's *Metamorphoses*, a group of stories loosely linked together but which make the same point; he often puts one after another several anecdotes or quotations which are not in any logical sequence but which in their way all imply a certain lesson or illuminate aspects of the problem he is treating; they thereby acquire a cumulative effect. The word oblique, which he himself uses, aptly describes the relations of the parts to the whole— 'se regardant, mais d'une vue oblique'—but a series of oblique lights on an object illuminate its complexity more fully than a light from one source. Such an open form may make the *Essais* more difficult to outline, but does not make them haphazard accumulations.

Some of the *Essais* are clearly organized; the central subject is easy to define and the relevance of the parts to the whole presents no problem. Others, such as II, xi or III, v, at first sight seem much less well organized and it is hard for the reader to see what holds them together. Yet Pierre

Villey worked out a very logical order from the lengthy *Apologie*, which goes in depth, destroying one by one every vestige of intellectual pride. Mr. Villey has also suggested the principles of organization of III, vi, *Des coches*, which is one of the most seemingly disorganized. Others have done the same with *De l'expérience*, etc. The most difficult problem is presented by the conclusions; Montaigne often leaves the essay open rather than providing a clear summary of the consequences of what he has been saying. Instead, the chapter ends abruptly on an afterthought. The sequence sometimes goes from the superficial to the profound aspects of the problem, or else becomes more and more personal—moving from universal considerations to those which particularly touch Montaigne. Otherwise, the move is generally from didactic to illustrative material. But to understand this order, we must understand the essay; we must understand how Montaigne thinks, what he means by the words he uses, and how he moves from one theme to another—what he considers the relation between them. In I, xlii, for instance, he casually moves from proving that riches are useless without good health to demonstrating that it is better to follow than to command; but these are both apt illustrations of his central point, that one should not be too attached to outside, material things. The more fully we understand Montaigne, the better organized he seems to be and the more relevant the parts seem to the whole.

*   *   *

Perhaps even more difficult, and more demanding of sensitivity on the reader's part, than the problem of order is the problem of tone. At the conclusion of I, l, Montaigne compares Democritus and Heraclitus. Both were aware that man's fate was vain, devoid of meaning and dignity—as Montaigne was. But whereas Heraclitus wept, Democritus laughed, and Montaigne preferred Democritus' attitude. Rather than uttering tragic complaints about life as he knew it, he insists that 'Nostre propre et peculière condition est autant ridicule que risible'. And he is often a comic author. Beholding the weaknesses of man, he laughs and wants to make us laugh.

Sometimes his laughter is the earthy laughter of the medieval fabliaux or of Rabelais. The woman from Toulouse to whom such remarkable things happen in the *Essais* is someone we have heard of in Chaucer or in a smoking car. There is an anecdote about human needs in I, xlii, which you can also find in Rabelais (*Quart livre*, lx); both borrowed it from Plutarch. Those digestive images which provide so much of

Montaigne's references also provide much of his humour. The venerability of the jokes in I, xxi, or indeed their Augustinian source, should help us appreciate this sort of comic, but should not make us overlook that earthy humour in Montaigne almost always serves to explode man's inflated ego; his purpose is to show that we cannot even control our own physical body, nor can we escape our condition. His objection to the pedant's fascination with dictionaries provokes the tale of a friend who 'n'oseroit me dire qu'il a le derriere galeux, s'il ne va sur le champ estudier en son lexicon, que c'est que galeux, et que c'est que derriere' (I, xxv). Here, Montaigne moves almost automatically to a comic, physical image which by juxtaposing reality with words effectively destroys the pretensions of the pedant. He so excels in telling comic anecdotes that we wish he indulged us more often. The stories are told with economy, and the comic twist is usually reserved to the end. Someone reproached for laying hands on a priest denies it, for 'il l'avoit battu et foulé aux pieds' (I, xli). This story takes Montaigne one sentence, and concludes the chapter on not boasting about your glory.

Montaigne also recalls Rabelais in his mastery of a purely verbal sort of comic. He enjoys inventing words which will have a comic effect. He was not above the pun, and often juxtaposes words which sound alike: 'marchandise . . . paillardise; nostre apercevance est obscure et obtuse; connoissance des choses . . . conduite des causes; la vérité nue et crue; la force, le fer, et le feu; monstre et miracle; aussi bien à rejeter qu'à recevoir' to quote a few examples from the beginning of III, xi. Usually these couples serve to emphasize his idea; often they lend themselves to his antithetical way of thinking; sometimes the combination provokes an unexpected meaning. Above all, his delight in assonance suggests the pleasure he took in writing, and his desire to amuse as well as instruct. Nor did his objections to rhetoric keep him from indulging in those long lists of words—one of verbs is especially remarkable—which Rabelais provides so often.

He is ironic in the sense that he says one thing while wishing to make us understand another. His use of 'beau', 'belle' to modify something he is attacking ('la belle science') gives the trick away. Such irony is most evident in the *Apologie*, where he constantly states in an exaggerated form those arguments with which he does not agree. The whole discussion of man's alleged superiority to animals more than borders on sarcasm. Finally what is normally considered good becomes bad, the bad good, and Montaigne's irony takes on antithetical form: 'La foiblesse de nostre jugement nous y ayde plus que la force, et nostre aveuglement plus que nostre clervoyance. C'est par l'entremise de nostre ignorance plus que de nostre science que nous sommes sçavans.' Words have a value which is the opposite of that usually given them; throughout Montaigne, such terms as *glory*, *knowledge*, *science* are used in a sarcastic sense. His irony, however, is not ambiguous; he never leaves us in doubt about where he stands. He uses comic sarcasm as a weapon because he believes the comic attitude towards life is the best attitude to take. Read, for instance, II, xxvii, with its attack on the medical profession. The list of gross remedies, the satire on the secrecy and the pretentiousness of doctors are obviously meant to provoke laughter. But the same chapter contains serious suggestions about the need for specialization and for medical records, and reflections of the physical pain Montaigne himself knew and his sincere desire for relief. The comic in Montaigne never destroys the seriousness of the *Essais*; it serves, instead, to make the point more effectively, and to prevent the rather despondent vision of life they contain from being a really tragic vision.

The comic also serves to enhance our pleasure in reading the *Essais*. The wry opening of III, vii, *De l'incommodité de la grandeur*: 'Puisque nous ne la pouvons aveindre, vengeons nous a en mesdire' is only matched by the conclusion of I, xxi, on the cannibals. After extolling their virtues, Montaigne adds: 'Tout cela ne va pas trop mal: mais quoy, ils ne portent point de haut de chausses!' The understatement of 'pas trop mal', combined with the sarcasm of the complaint about their undressed state, directed not of course at the cannibals but at the European's standard of values, is both broad and subtle. This bemused humour only makes Montaigne's point more effective. To understand the man, we must be aware of this comic and enjoy it.

* * *

Montaigne is also a teller of stories, and much of his charm stems from the many anecdotes which pepper the pages of the *Essais*. Not that he is a Boccaccio or a Marguerite de Navarre who missed his vocation; the stories are usually an integral part of the *Essais* and serve, the way the quotations do, to make a point Montaigne considers important. Also, although he seems at times quite fascinated with the stories, he usually tells them in a rather non-dramatic manner, in the third person, which helps underline the didactic point. He pares the descriptive detail to a bare minimum. Montaigne gives us enough information to make the story realistic, but not enough to move us into the world of fiction, and the anecdote remains illustrative, enjoyable as it may be. The stories serve the purpose parables do in the Gospels, or anecdotes in a lecture: they fix the point, and bring it dramatically home to the reader.

Some of them are quite long, and provide the meat of an essay. For instance, in II, xxxvii, there are two very detailed stories—about how a village lost its innocence, and about a goat with the stone—whose point always remains apparent but which are so fully developed that the former could find its place in a travel volume, the latter in a collection on the monstrosities of nature. Other anecdotes take only two or three sentences, and simply evoke a situation which proves Montaigne's point, or render concrete what might otherwise be too abstract.

They also come from a variety of sources. Some Montaigne borrows from other authors, especially from Latin historians; some come from the folk tradition; some from his own experience. There is no way of knowing how he improves on this last group by adding details and sacrificing accuracy for effectiveness the way any good story-teller must, but we can see how he changes the anecdotes he derives from classical sources. Villey's large critical edition will not only tell you where the story is from, but even often give the source text; by setting this alongside Montaigne's version much can be learned about his art as a story-teller, about how his mind worked and about his style.

Montaigne treats sources in two radically different ways. Sometimes he adapts very freely; it is as if he read an anecdote in Amyot's Plutarch, and then a week later sat down to recount the same tale in his own words and manner. In other instances, he follows his source closely and obviously had it in front of him as he wrote; what he comes up with is almost a translation, but a translation which freely suppresses or augments. The first group tells us much about his narrative technique; the second throws some light on him as a story-teller, but is even more informative about his style. Curiously, Montaigne often seems most completely himself when he is following his source closely. For instance, in I, xxiv, the anecdote about Augustus and Cinna is told in a manner which is vivacious, hardly Latin, and redolent of Montaigne; we hear him speak in every word. Yet, if you compare it to the Senecan original (see below), you will have to exercise some finesse to find how and where he has changed the original.

Joseph Vianey has studied his adaptation of material in four instances, from Livy, Plutarch-Amyot, Lopez de Gomara and Justus Lipsius. Montaigne puts off using direct quotations until he gets to the really dramatic moment; then, he is more concerned than his source with using a realistic vocabulary. He suppresses much specific detail in order to emphasize emotions and feelings. He cuts down on the preliminary material so he can immediately get to the heart of the action, and suppresses picturesque details which slow down the story and detract interest from its hero; he emphasizes psychological traits. Montaigne is almost a seventeenth-century author in his preference for rapid action, his desire to describe not events but personalities, and his concentration on one individual. With Lopez de Gomara, he makes more basic adjustments; he suppresses some details and adds others borrowed from elsewhere—particularly affective details which will make the anecdote more vivid. Whereas with Amyot he suppresses the superfluous, here he augments a rather sparse source. In the case of Justus Lipsius, Vianey studies not how Montaigne borrows an anecdote but how he gets from his source his description of an amphitheatre. Lipsius read all available documents, summarized and compared them; from this great wealth of material Montaigne, obviously working from memory, draws a brief tableau with a few effective, salient details. Again, his technique varies according to his source and his need; but his changes tend to make the action more dramatic, more psychological, and (surprising as this may seem) he suppresses, rather than adds details.

Let us look at three brief anecdotes where Montaigne follows his source quite closely. The first is the tale in II, xxxi, about Plutarch's philosophical slave who objected to being whipped, borrowed from Aulus Gellius. The changes seem few, but they tell us much about his art. His goal is dramatic intensity, and he achieves it by using interrogatives ('neque in spuman ruboremque effervesco' becomes 'Rougisje? écumé-je?'); he intensifies adverbs and substitutes precise, specific ones for general, abstract ones ('lente et leniter' becomes 'tout froidement et tout rassis'); he adds colourful interjections ('rustre'). At the same time, he makes the story flow more smoothly by suppressing repetitious and irrelevant details (in Aulus Gellius, the slave gives the title of Plutarch's book against anger; Montaigne also combines several verbs into one, omits narrative detail). Or he simplifies radically the sentence-structure of his source: 'All those things which were written in his book in no wise he followed' becomes 'démentait entièrement ses écrits'. Often he combines several sentences into one, thereby emphasizing the continuity of the action.

In II, xxiv, Montaigne recounts the story of how Antiochus, the Seleucid king, submitted to the commands of Popilius and abandoned his successful programme of conquest. Montaigne found the story in Livy (XLV, xii–xiii). Here, the changes are very obvious; Montaigne omits a long passage, some twenty lines, which tells of further activities of Antiochus and other contemporary events, and replaces it by his own moral generalization ('Avoir renoncé à une si grande monarchie . . .'). He concludes the anecdote in a way which only loosely follows his

source. He also introduces proper names and pronouns to increase
clarity, and suppresses several unimportant details. The changes again
serve to emphasize the lesson he wishes to make, or to render his narrative
more economical and effective. Those who see in Montaigne a prolix and
uneconomical writer must keep in mind that he eliminates much from
his sources and adds only what is dramatically or didactically pertinent.

On occasion, though, the changes by which he makes a source his
own are a good deal more subtle. Take the story in I, xxiv, where
Augustus pardons Cinna, which is borrowed from Seneca. At first
sight, Montaigne seems to follow his source quite closely. Yet again, he
eliminates. The details about how Augustus discovered the plot disappear,
as do several psychological details, because Montaigne wants to insist
on the sudden transformation of Augustus' character. The picturesque
Latin: 'I am a head exposed to noble adolescents, on which they sharpen
their swords' also goes, because Montaigne thought it not consonant
with Augustus' character. Livia's vague reference to the many other
conspirators her husband has killed is dropped, because Montaigne
prefers the specific. He omits adverbs of time and colourless adjectives.
The original statement that to repeat all of Augustus' speech would
take several volumes becomes simply 'après plusieurs autres propos';
Montaigne found the Latin exaggerated and irrelevant. He also suppresses 'aun hanc poenam, qua sola erat contentus futurus, extenderet',
and moves directly into a statement of what the punishment is to be.
These are the more important of many suppressions. Some serve to
tighten the story by getting rid of extraneous details; Montaigne is even
willing to sacrifice the picturesque. Others perceptibly make Augustus
more totally converted to a new approach than he is in the original.

Montaigne changes much less than he suppresses, and the changes are
usually made for the sake of clarity or to heighten dramatic effect; on
the whole, he takes only those liberties a good translator might be
permitted. The Latin 'tarried' becomes simply 'estant'; the more
abstract verb is necessary because the story is separated from its original
context. (Montaigne frequently substitutes a participle for a Latin
clause, thereby achieving a better subordination of elements.) Elsewhere, he prefers a more violent verb and translates 'struere' by the
strong colloquial 'brasser'. Only when seeking such colloquial effects
does he weaken the Latin. At times he reverses the original order to
achieve a more effective sequence. He again turns statements, particularly
accusations, into questions, and frequently joins two sentences into one,
replacing a period with an *et*; the Senecan amble ambles even more in
Montaigne. In the Latin, Augustus asks Cinna 'not to interrupt me

when I am speaking, not to speak in the middle of my discourse' which simply becomes 'n'interrons pas mon parler'—combining the suppression of unimportant detail with a quest for colloquialism.

Aside from these changes, Montaigne adds very little to his source. Usually the additions increase the clarity of the narrative; 'manda *pour cet effect au lendemain*', or the whole sentence explaining that Augustus was to be killed as he was making a sacrifice. Sometimes he doubles an affective word ('clementia' becomes 'la douceur et la clemence') or even a sentence: 'Et se despartit d'avec luy en cette maniere.' Only with the last sentence does he really augment his source, adding both details which locate the event and his own moral judgment on the story.

The frame of the story is changed more radically than its actual 'plot', which suggests that Montaigne was concerned with blending the anecdote in with the essay and making it apposite. He wants to achieve not only clarity but also a colloquial vividness; otherwise, he is impatient with irrelevancies and details. These revisions do not suggest a luxuriant imagination; rather, they suggest a forceful, didactic mind, which tells stories not just for the pleasure of telling them, but in order to persuade.

* * *

These comparisons offer some insight into Montaigne's prose style, which always seems remarkably unique. He is like certain painters, whose works you immediately recognize even if the subject of the picture is one you have never seen him treat before; we hear Montaigne's own voice speak on every page of the *Essais*. Yet this style, like any style, is hard to define. It is easy to be impressionistic about it and term it 'casual' or 'conversational', but it is difficult to describe it precisely. A close analysis of certain passages, a comparison with his sources, the study of his revisions, the cataloguing of certain devices, together with an awareness of the historical problems presented by style at his time, could permit such a definition. Some of this work has been done by Maurice Croll (especially on the historical problem), R. A. Sayce, Albert Thibaudet, and most systematically by Floyd Gray. What follows is largely a résumé of what they have observed with a few suggestions of my own. To facilitate illustrating, I quote a brief passage from III, xii (as it appeared in the 1595 edition) to the lines of which the numbered references refer:

1 Comme quelqu'vn pourroit dire de moy: que i'ay seulement faict icy vn amas de fleurs estrangeres, n'y ayant

fourny du mien, que le filet à les lier. Certes i'ay
donné à l'opinion publique, que ces parements empruntez
5 m'accompaignent: mais ie n'entends pas qu'ils me cou-
urent, & qu'ils me cachent; c'est le rebours de mon
dessein. Qui ne veux faire montre que du mien & de ce
qui est mien par nature. Et si ie m'en fusse creu, à
tout hazard, i'eusse parlé tout fin seul. Ie m'en charge
10 de plus fort, tous les iours, outre ma proposition & ma
forme premiere, sur la fantasie du siecle: & par oisi-
ueté. S'il me messied à moy, comme ie le croy, n'importe:
il peut estre vtile à quelque autre. Tel allegue Platon
& Homere, qui ne les vid onques: & moy, ay prins des
15 lieux assez, ailleurs qu'en leur source. Sans peine &
sans suffisance, ayant mille volumes de liures, autour
de moy, en ce lieu où i'escris, i'emprunteray presente-
ment s'il me plaist, d'vne douzaine de tels rauaudeurs,
gens que ie ne fueillette guere, deqouy esmailler le
20 traicté de la Physionomie. Il ne faut que l'epitre li-
minaire d'vn Allemand pour me farcir d'allegations: &
nous allons quester par là vne friande gloire, à piper
le sot monde.

To begin with, the 'genre' of the *Essais* is hard to define. Historically, some (indeed, most) essays are definitely didactic, hopefully convincing presentations of a point of view. Other essays are much more conversational, casual in their structure, and try to convince by other than purely logical means; indeed, essays may even take dialogue or dramatic form. Montaigne is always both conversational and didactic, and this dichotomy must be remembered in discussing his style. The essays are fundamentally pedagogical; Montaigne may claim he is reciting man and not forming him, but he none the less wrote a whole chapter on how a young man should be formed. He distinguishes between books which please and books which teach, and his own is obviously intended to teach. His opposition to certain forms of zealous dogmatism should not make us overlook how concerned he is with stating the 'pheno-menology of morality' accurately, with attacking certain forms of behaviour and propounding others.

Yet, the tone could just as well be described as conversational; Montaigne preferred conversation to reading. He was a social animal, and would have written to one individual rather than for an abstract general public (if La Boétie had not died!); indeed, he seems to have written primarily with a select group of acquaintances in mind. Often, when he does address the reader, he uses the intimate *tu* form. He asserts that his style is a 'style parlé'—'Je parle au papier comme je parle au premier que je rencontre.' He is opposed to 'le bien dire pur', the somewhat artificial style used by most of his contemporaries, and would rather imitate the language of the public markets with its freshness and simplicity.

Keeping this dichotomy in mind, we can proceed to define his style, first in terms of what it is not, for he avoids certain sorts of artifice even though he practises others; then in terms of what it is—a style which aims for and achieves values of continuity, totality and vividness.

His style avoids not only the neologisms which characterize Rabelais but also the extensive, complicated conceits of many Renaissance prose-writers. More importantly, Montaigne wilfully and publicly turns his back on the complicated, tightly organized Ciceronian sentence. His revolt against the humanism of the early Renaissance led him to reject an overly intellectual and imitative style, to prefer the 'soldatesque' style of Caesar or the 'disorderly' style of Seneca to the rhetorical style of Cicero. He sought a personal style which would allow the expression of individual character. This is what he terms a natural style—one which is true to your nature, and not one which is unplanned or uncontrolled; for Montaigne did revise his writings, and usually with happy results (19: *esmailler* for earlier *enrichir*). Montaigne was as much at home in Latin as in French, but this anti-Ciceronian attitude helped make him choose to use the vernacular. The Ciceronian period is easy enough in a highly inflected language, but difficult in French where the more resolved style of a Seneca or a Tacitus could be imitated with profit and ease. So he wrote a free and open style, to fit his open form; indeed, he not only wrote incomplete sentences but even used pronouns without antecedents (7, *Qui*).

But this anti-Ciceronianism does not mean that Montaigne wrote in a sloppy, uncontrolled way, for he clearly strove after certain qualities. The first of these might be called continuity. This is manifest in his punctuation; he does not even paragraph, but lets his thought flow on from sentence to sentence through the essay. When he does punctuate, it is not to indicate the end of a thought unit, but in a way quite his own, to add emphasis or accentuate. He begins many of his sentences with co-ordinate conjunctions, especially *et* (8) which had a stronger meaning in his day than now and usually indicates a progression in his thought rather than a simple linking (9, 11, 21), and which peppers his prose. Other connecting words (*selon, aussi, par ainsin*) are also frequent.

As a result, every sentence is bound to the one before it and to the one after, and so to speak is open at both ends. Deciding when a sentence starts or finishes is often purely arbitrary, and Montaigne's editors have understandably arrived at different punctuations. Finally, to create this sense of continuity, he uses a great many present participles (16, 2), especially in A. These participles, together with his interpolation of sentences in the present tense when he is recounting something which took place in the past (and, indeed, his constant mixing of present, past and future verbs), make us feel that the thought is unfolding before our eyes.

Montaigne's style is also a total style. He does not follow any strict rules about what goes where, what sort of language he has to use or what kind of length of sentence he may write. As a result, he could employ a wide variety of style levels with the greatest of ease. There are passages which are extremely colloquial and personal; others are rhetorical and serious; some are almost precious. In his brief dedication to Mme de Grammont in I, xxix, he deftly combines a courtly, flattering language with informal, almost comic elements—without creating an ironic effect. Our example combines such colloquialisms as 'piper le sot monde' with the evocation of Plato and Homer. He combines very common verbs with very colourful ones. The variety of tone is reflected in the rhythm; some passages move slowly, others very rapidly. As we noted in discussing his comic tone, he does not hesitate to use onomatopoeia, assonance, alliteration, or even puns; he is very conscious of the possibilities of the sound of language (5–6; 16).

His style is a total one in another more striking sense; though, as we noted in studying his adaptation of Latin sources, he often suppresses irrelevant detail, he tries always to catch every shading of his thought, every important aspect of whatever he is discussing. As a result, he tends to double and even triple his adjectives, his verbs (5–6), or other descriptive elements (10–11). A compulsion to get everything down leads to an accumulation of co-ordinate expressions. Or, indeed, of subordinate ones; Montaigne frequently introduces parenthetical elements in his effort to seize the whole of the *passage*, rather than to catch any oversimplified *essence*. He uses parenthetical clauses (12, 17, 18, 19), introduces words between subject and verb, between *pour* and infinitive. The 'C'est . . . que' or 'c'est . . . un' constructions are almost his trademark. He unexpectedly adds an adjective at the end of a sentence (11). The result is to give the reader the feeling that Montaigne has investigated and expressed every possible aspect of his subject.

Finally, and most central, his style aims at creating graphic, vivid effects. We have already mentioned his verbs; often he uses vivid ones which are descriptive and laden with adjectival qualities. In our brief passage we find *couvrir, cacher, messeoir, alleguer, emprunter, feuilleter, esmailler, farcir, quêter* and *piper*; from this list alone you can almost guess what the passage is about. He particularly likes verbs which make us see the action going on; and he enjoys using such verbs in a figurative sense (*émailler, farcir*). He also makes frequent use of intensifiers, not only superlatives and such forms as *très*, but also the adverbial *tout* (9), *si, tel* (18), *même*; he intensifies pronouns with disjunctive forms (12, 14), there perhaps in part compensating for his lax syntax. Other devices serve to reinforce and emphasize his thought: rhetorical questions, exclamatory sentences (particularly at the beginning or end of a development), and interjections. His graphic style is most manifest, however, in his imagery, with all its vivid evocations. Montaigne, by adding a verb, or an adjective, or a clause, is always moving from the general to the particular —and he does this above all by his images.

Albert Thibaudet, Gilbert Mayer and Floyd Gray have analysed this imagery in an effort to measure its literary effectiveness and to discover how Montaigne's imagination worked. He rarely uses explicit forms of comparison. In I, xxvi, Mayer counted some seventy-seven metaphors, of which only four took the form of similes; Gray suggests that there are only around a hundred similes in all the *Essais*. These are usually from the 1580 text, and evidently represent a conscious effort to do what authors ought to do. Yet, very few of these are derived from mythological or literary sources; rather, they come from Montaigne's own experience and, as is also true with the imagery, they serve not to explain but to extend his thought; they may even provoke a transition.

Indeed, the salient feature of his imagery is that it serves not so much to illustrate his thought as to express it. Montaigne moves right into the image; he suppresses such words as *comme* or *ainsi que*, and establishes equivalences between image and non-image world. In our text, speaking of his use of quotations, he says he could easily find 'de quoy esmailler le traicté'; he does not say 'to embellish as if by enamel work' but 'to enamel the treatise'. The image, as so often with Montaigne, is expressed through the verb, not through a noun, which suggests how natural the metaphorical way of thinking was for him. As a result, the reader on occasion has difficulty distinguishing between what is image and what is direct statement; when Montaigne speaks of borrowed quotations as flowers or jewels, and then goes on to say he does not want them to hide or cover him, we sense not that he is using illustrations, but that this is the way he thinks about the abuse of quotations. Here, he resembles a poet more than he does a prose-essayist. Montaigne always considers abstractions concretely, and the reader tends to lose sight of the abstract and become conscious only of the concrete.

Once, when Thibaudet was ill and incapable of any more arduous task, he drew up a catalogue of Montaigne's images. He divided them into four groups: those which contrast interior with exterior, those which deal with organic sensation, those which discuss movement and change, and those which are purely visual. Of these, the last are few in number and of little importance except that they show Montaigne's attempts to imitate a style of prose common in his age. The images concerned with outside and inside draw on the relations between body and soul, between body and clothes, on buildings, on the dyeing of cloth. Those which deal with organic sensation evoke weight, qualities of thickness or viscosity, sickness, food, vegetal growth, and contact of the body with the outside. But by far the most numerous are the images of motion and change. Indeed, often the outside–inside images describe a movement from the one to the other, and the images of organic sensation imply motion, fluidity, digestion, etc. Many images are derived from walking or riding on horseback, hunting or racing, or from more general qualities of elasticity and torsion. About half the images imply change of some sort.

So we must conclude that the 'branle du Caucase' was not a striking image found by Montaigne to support a temporary philosophical point. We could, thinking in polar terms as he was accustomed to do, divide people into those who conceive of the world as something stable and those who always see motion—who, when looking at a parked motor car, see it driving down the street. Montaigne is at the extreme limit of this second group; everywhere he looks, he sees motion and change. But Thibaudet's catalogue does not tell us precisely what value he attached to change; an analysis of several images suggests that it could be good or bad, but it would be of great interest to know under which circumstances motion was seen as dangerous, under which as salutary. The problem is not a simple one. Take the outside–inside images; on the one hand, Montaigne wants to struggle against any pressure from the outside, to present an impermeable surface which will resist all attacks; on the other, he recognizes that the price to be paid for such resistance is an incapacity to move, a lack of *souplesse*, which he regards as regrettable. We cannot close the question by saying that he sought an equilibrium between these two tendencies; it is precisely here that Montaigne becomes a most challenging author to analyse.

Many metaphors deal with clothing; usually, clothing is equated with the artificial, which also restrains motion, whereas to disrobe is to become both more mobile and more natural. The numerous images of facial expression and the mask also contrast a natural face and a made-up face. The metaphors of dyeing are rather different; there, something applied on the outside gradually penetrates inside, and the natural changes definitions; these metaphors express Montaigne's belief that man could change, provided the change, through habit, became ingrained. Indeed, many of the images could be divided into those in which digestion or absorption of some sort takes place, and those in which only a passing and usually a restricting contact is made between one substance and another. Some of the food imagery, for instance, emphasizes digestion and absorption, others passage and elimination. Similarly, when describing exterior objects, he calls attention to the smooth, polished separateness of some, as opposed to the rough and penetrating qualities of others. The rough contact, which will permit absorption, is usually preferred, but only if absorption is possible.

Many images suggest that Montaigne associated the sensation of life with the sensation or at least the possibility of motion. He frequently opposes the fluid to the solid, or indicates the degree of viscosity. Montaigne liked to think while walking or riding on horseback, and associates motion with honest thinking. More complicated is the contrast between regular and irregular motion; the former often suggests a purely natural being, but may imply indifference and be equated with immobility; the latter may suggest the imposed unnatural, but also the possibility of change. As is his thought, Montaigne's images are polar; but the poles shift frequently. There is an opposition between roughness (absorbable) and smoothness (indifferent); there is another one between mobility (good) and immobility (bad), and yet another between inside-out (good) and outside-in (usually bad); any categorization of the metaphors by subject-matter runs afoul of these series of poles. Others can easily be discovered; motion is often considered in up–down terms; rising is good, unless it indicates pride, and the same ambiguity holds for descending. The circle for Montaigne is not the image of completion and accomplishment, but rather of uselessness and incoherency. Close study should be paid to his images of water. For him, water comes near to being reality itself in its mobile essence, the substance which resists but flees, and hence the image of that complexity with which Montaigne struggled all his life. And yet he never speaks of the beauty of a lake or of a waterfall.

Many categories of imagery which are highly significant in other authors are meaningless in Montaigne. When he speaks of fire and light, he is concerned with their movement, not their brightness or heat; although he was very sensitive to smells, his olfactory images are rare. His references to music and sculpture are generally superficial borrowings from other authors. But as a Renaissance prose-writer he possessed a freedom at composing his own metaphors, even when that freedom led to logical incoherence, and Renaissance prose tended to be highly figurative if not mannerist. The frequency and importance of imagery in Montaigne may in part be explained by the history of prose; it is not entirely a matter of his thinking in metaphorical terms, but that writers of his time dressed their discourses with figures, and the figures were less set than they were to be a century later. As a result, Montaigne's metaphors are as susceptible of analysis as are those of a Romantic poet, and thus more light can be gained from reading a passage in terms of how he says something than in terms of what he says. Indeed, our brief study of his images has coincided with what we had earlier observed about the *branle*, the *naturel*, the antithesis, and other aspects of his thought. Mr. Gray maintains that it is the organic growth of these images which most often gives to an essay its unity, and R. H. Sayce has impressively demonstrated how this is so in *Des coches*. Certainly, to appreciate Montaigne you must not read him casually in order to catch a few bright ideas, or rapidly try to make an outline of his 'great thoughts', but slowly, sensing the multiple aspects of what he is discussing, grasping his thought in its rich and often complex continuity, and appreciating the vivid, forceful manner in which, despite his refusal of certain forms of assertiveness, he managed to write so well.

Further Reading

The most convenient text of the *Essais* is Albert Thibaudet's Pléïade edition. The studies of Pierre Villey, especially *Les sources et l'évolution des Essais de Montaigne*, remain essential. The most recent, and best general study in English is Donald Frame's *Montaigne's Discovery of Man* (1955); Hugo Friedrich's *Montaigne* (1949; in German) is penetrating and exhaustive. Albert Thibaudet's posthumous *Montaigne* (1963) is difficult to use but thought-provoking. On the period in general, Hiram Haydn's *The Counter Renaissance* (1950) helps place Montaigne.

More specialized studies which raise important critical problems include: Maurice Croll, 'Attic Prose: Lipsius, Montaigne, Bacon' in *Schelling Anniversary Papers*, 1923; Joseph Vianey, 'Montaigne conteur' in *Mélanges de philologie et d'histoire offerts à Edmond Huguet*, 1940; W. G. Moore, 'Montaigne's Notion of Experience' in *The French Mind, Studies in honor of Gustave Rudler*, 1952; R. A. Sayce, 'Baroque Elements in Montaigne' in *French Studies*, VIII (1954), 1–16; and finally Floyd Gray, *Le style de Montaigne* (1958), which contains a useful bibliography.